A new life for the little dog wh

THE
LONG WAY
HOME

Sometimes one lifetime just isn't enough

Martina Mars

First published in Great Britain in 2023 by Addendum Publishing
www.addendumpublishing.co.uk

ISBN 978-1-8383675-2-7

Cover design by BespokeBookCovers.com
All photos & images, including cover photos, author's own collection.

For Polo

Thanks for… everything

CONTENTS

Chapter 1

A NEW BEGINNING

The first thing I remembered was the music. That and the feeling of being loved. And for the longest time those were the only things I remembered.

You see, the thing about coming back from the Other Side and being born again is that you forget. They told me it's made that way so you can be free to do so something completely different. Otherwise all you would do is remember your former life and what went on before, and you would be stuck with all the old memories and what happened back in your last life and you wouldn't be able to move on.

Also, come to think about it, there would really be no point in doing the same thing all over again. Coming back is all about learning and growing and doing something completely new. At least that's what they told me when I was still over on the

Other Side.

Only for me it was also about finding my parents again. Because I love them very, very much, and I missed them an awful lot after I died. The same way they loved and missed me, too.

Not sure if you remember, but I once told you that my mum believes, when you truly love someone, and they love you right back the exact same way, your souls become entwined and are linked forever by an unbreakable bond. Sort of like an invisible rubber band that goes from your soul to the one you love. And all you need to do if you want to find them again, is to make a wish and trust the link to pull you right back to them.

I'm not completely sure if it's *strictly* allowed, and I reckon it doesn't really happen all that often because of the whole forgetting-stuff-as-soon-as-you-are-born-again thing, but I'm quite stubborn if you recall.

By the way, it doesn't matter who or what you are either – dog, human, horse, mouse, rat, *even* cat… Anyway, you're getting my drift. Love is love.

And that's exactly what happened with me and my parents. Didn't matter one iota that they are human and I am a dog.

The only problem was that as soon as I was born again, I couldn't remember A THING. Nothing AT ALL about my former life.

I didn't remember my birth mother and siblings, nor did I remember the horrible time I had spent with the people who took me away from them and then promptly abandoned me at the rescue centre where my parents finally found and adopted me. I didn't remember my mum and my dad, who I love more than anyone in the whole wide world, nor any of my beloved aunts and uncles. I also didn't remember the house by the sea that was my *Home*, nor any of my MANY rules and routines. Not even my Rule Number One, DON'T TOUCH MY BOTTOM! OR MY BACK! – can you believe it?!!

I didn't even remember my own name!

I didn't remember dying either, and finding out that I was still very much alive, only on the Other Side. And I didn't remember that I had tried so hard to fix all my precious memories firmly in my heart and mind and told myself to REMEMBER, before I let the link pull me right back to my parents.

I only felt that something important was missing and I just couldn't figure out what that something was. But all the time I had this urgent feeling that I *should* remember something but just couldn't.

And so I kept wandering about, doing the usual puppy things – you know, like running around, jumping up at everything and everyone, nipping my siblings, peeing and pooing everywhere, doing my damnedest to chew the furniture and everything else in sight to a pulp and trying my hardest to wreck the place. But something kept niggling at the back of my brain, and every time someone picked me up and gazed lovingly into my eyes it just didn't seem *right*. Don't get me wrong, they were lovely people, but they were just not MY people. And deep down, even though I didn't remember my family, I just *knew*.

The other HUGE problem with following the link that pulls you back to the people you love, is that nobody seems to have taken the 'where' into account when they thought of it.

You see, by the time I had finally figured out how to come back to your side of things, my parents weren't at home. Only I didn't know this.

So, on that day when I made my wish and trusted the link to pull me right back to them like they had taught me to, it pulled me there alright.

The only problem was that my mum and dad happened to be abroad on holidays at the time, in Argentina to be precise, visiting my Auntie Pachy, my dad's sister who lives in Buenos Aires. But unfortunately for me, by the time I found my bearings again, they were long gone, back home to the UK.

And that's how I got stranded in Argentina, a country I had never been to before. Sure, I understood most of the lingo. After all, my parents had taught me plenty of Spanish words during my last life. And I picked up the rest in no time at all. I'm not slow, you know! Unfortunately that didn't help me one little bit, because not only had I forgotten all about my old life, but the people I ended up with didn't speak any dog. And so, by the time I *did* remember, I couldn't explain to anyone what had happened and where I needed to be.

What also doesn't help matters of course is the fact that humans always tend to think they have to take care of you, which makes it rather hard to make your own decisions and to go places by yourself.

But I'm getting ahead of myself. Let me tell you what happened.

I don't actually remember *being* born again. But I do remember it being dark and warm and that there were a lot of us. Oh, and being hungry. *Very* hungry… ALL THE TIME!! And scrabbling around and fighting for the best spot to suck and eat. I also remember being licked all over from top to toe, and especially at the rear end. And of course, snoozing endlessly in between.

I think that's also when I first remembered the music. It popped up right in the middle of one of my puppy dreams and never left again. I just didn't know what it meant and where it came from, but it wrapped itself right around me and made me feel loved and *Home*.

The first few weeks of my life went by in a rather comfy haze, and the next thing I remember is being picked up by a woman who called herself La Tía. She was the first human person I saw when I could open my eyes at last. She was also the one who took me and my brothers and sisters away from our mother one day without telling us why. And without letting us say goodbye.

I guess La Tía was nice enough, because she always made sure we had plenty of food to eat and toys to play with. But she didn't exactly hang out with us. And she made us have baths and gave us strange medicines which wasn't great.

Then, after a while, there were suddenly lots of

people who came to visit us. Almost every day. They cooed and played with us and stroked us A LOT. They were on the whole a friendly bunch and let us lick their faces. They didn't take to being nipped that much though, but hey, they just had to put up with it.

Then, another little while later, I noticed whenever we had visitors, one or two of them seemed to forget to put my siblings back down before they left. I saw them walk off with them and never come back. La Tía didn't seem to notice. It was most peculiar. So every day there were less of us. She still didn't seem to notice. But I was beginning to wonder if maybe she just didn't care. Of course I soon learned what all that was about.

🐕

One day a man turned up all by himself. Unlike all the other visitors before him he didn't spend much time oohing and aahing and especially not *awwwwwwwing*. And he made it very clear that face licking wasn't on the menu. Nor was playing. He just picked me up unceremoniously, turned me over, inspected my bits and my teeth and in general treated me as if I was one of our stuffed toys.

Luckily for him I hadn't remembered yet who I

was. And so I let him give me the undignified once-over – although my lips *had* begun to quiver mightily and to expose a sharp set of what my mum would have called 'first edition pearly whites'.

However, just before I could try them out on him, he plonked me back down on the floor once more, and I heard him tell La Tía that he wanted to buy me as a Christmas present for his girlfriend. I guess that was why he had been inspecting the goods – to make sure there was nothing missing before he bought me.

I didn't really want to go with him. Nor did I particularly want to be a Christmas present either. But I wasn't given a choice in the matter. The man handed La Tía a wad of money, and she handed me over to him in exchange. Wrapped in a blanket so I couldn't object. Or move for that matter.

I didn't get a chance to say goodbye to anyone either, and that's when I finally understood what had happened to all my other siblings before me.

My mum always used to say that a lot of Christmas presents aren't exactly of the 'wanted' variety. Turns out, neither was I. Not completely anyhow.

When I was finally presented to the man's

girlfriend – inside a cardboard box under the Christmas tree, with a frilly ribbon around my neck and a dozen little pink hearts dangling from it – I kid you not! – she took one look at me and, as I looked right back at her, we both realised we weren't exactly what we had expected of each other.

But the deal had been done. And we both made do. Me because I didn't have a choice. And she because she didn't want to upset her man.

She lifted me out of my box, pretended she was as over the moon about seeing me as I was about finally getting out of the stupid box I had been sitting in for ages, and put me down.

My legs were decidedly wobbly from having to sit for so long, but I soon raced along to explore my new abode. The floor was all tiles and very slippery, and my legs went right out from under me each time I skidded round the many corners.

The place was bigger than La Tía's had been, with more rooms I could get into, but to my utter disappointment I couldn't find any toys anywhere. Nor was there anything else to chew on, and the furniture was way too high for me to jump up on. Most annoying!

In the end I got bored running around and exploring all by myself and fell asleep on the floor while The Girlfriend and her man were busy licking each other's faces in the other room.

All in all I wasn't too impressed with where I had ended up at. The only good thing was that I had a real tree to mark at last, instead of the wads of newspaper back at La Tía's. Well, okay, only until the man and his girlfriend noticed. Then all hell broke loose, I got an almighty talking to, and peeing up the Christmas tree henceforth was a thing of the past.

The next morning The Girlfriend bought me my first collar and lead – which I could have done without! – and a doggie bed and some plastic toys I was allowed to chew on. The latter admittedly only after a *little* incident involving The Girlfriend's favourite shoes and… um… my teeth, during which I got told ONCE AND FOR ALL that The Girlfriend's things were COMPLETELY OUT OF BOUNDS as far as I was concerned. And let me tell you, she raised her voice *quite* sufficiently for me to get it. At once.

After that life settled into a rather dull routine very fast. The Girlfriend decided to call me Benito which didn't exactly feel right. But since I didn't know why, and because I couldn't tell her so, I put up with it.

She also taught me how to behave and what to do and when, and especially what NOT to do. And I mostly complied. Because the food was good. So much better than what I had been given at La Tía's.

And, yes, okay, because I didn't know any better. Yet.

The Girlfriend also introduced me to the vet. Which wasn't necessary because I was perfectly healthy and didn't need any of the stuff he gave me. Nor did I need to be prodded and poked with needles, but of course him being a vet, he just couldn't help himself and did it anyway.

I'm not saying The Girlfriend was mean or anything, even though I didn't get to play that much anymore. She was just a bit indifferent and… well, boring if I'm honest. Of course The Girlfriend had a proper name, too, but I just couldn't be bothered to remember it. I kept thinking of her as The Girlfriend and that was that. I guess, something deep inside myself was even then telling me that I wasn't going to stick around forever.

I felt this urgency to be somewhere else all the time, without knowing why and where I needed to be. Only when I was dreaming did I come close to finding out, but each time I woke up I just couldn't remember again. Most frustrating! And I REALLY tried, believe you me!!

But, like I told you, I did remember the music. Whenever I closed my eyes I could hear it so clearly and it made me feel so happy and warm and loved inside. Which is why I ended up spending most of my time lazing around, snoozing, listening to the music inside my head and trying to figure out what the hell was going on and what I was meant to do next.

In the meantime, The Girlfriend told everyone that even though I wasn't the Chihuahua she had always wanted, I was the world's most easy-going dog. I didn't bother to correct her as she mostly left me in peace to do my own thing – i.e. sleeping and dreaming and eating, and sleeping and dreaming and eating some more.

We lived in an apartment on the 6th floor of a large building, surrounded by many, many other buildings, and to get to it we had to use the metal cage that swept up and down and made you feel like your stomach was popping in and out of your mouth. There was a staircase, too, but apart from the odd occasion we didn't use it because The Girlfriend simply HATED stairs. I'm just judging by the fuss she made on the few occasions we *had* to use them because apparently some *boludo* or other had left the door open on the first floor. Again!!

We had a simple routine together. The Girlfriend would get up late each morning, give me my breakfast whilst only having coffee herself (???!!!) – which unfortunately meant that I couldn't beg any extra food off her. Then she would get washed and dressed – which positively took AGES – and take me for my first walk of the day. Around the block of buildings and back again.

I made the most of the short walk by quickly marking my territory all along the way, and peeing and pooing in my favourite spot by a large tree that had grown out of a hole in the pavement.

After lunch The Girlfriend would watch the telly and/or paint her toe- and fingernails, which always made me sneeze and wonder why on earth she would bother to do so. After all, it didn't make her feet and fingers any more effective, as far as I could tell. Luckily she never attempted to paint mine. I have a funny feeling she wouldn't have found me quite so easy-going after all if she had…

When she was finally done with all her weird preening, The Girlfriend would spend endless hours on the phone whilst drinking *mate* tea by way of sucking it through a metal straw from a small wooden bowl type thing. Never figured out why she didn't drink it straight from the mug, the way she drank her coffee. But she wasn't the only one who had that strange habit. All her friends who popped over – and of course her man – did the same.

Humans are so strange!

In the evening, just after dinner and before we went to bed, The Girlfriend would take me for the last walk of the day. I used the time to thoroughly mark my territory once more, all around the block and back again.

I also accompanied The Girlfriend on her many shopping trips. And boy, did she like to shop! I began to wonder if there was anything left inside the shops she frequented. I had to stay outside most of the time, bored stiff waiting for her, tied to some fence or tree or post until eventually she would come back out again with TONS of shopping bags in her hands.

I met a few other dogs while I was waiting for her, but most of them were indifferent and didn't want to play or say hello. They seemed rather full of themselves – like their uppity parents. Which is why in the end I ignored them all as they walked past me. Pretended they weren't there and sniffed the air instead of their bottoms.

The Girlfriend's man didn't live with us, but he popped in plenty of times, and occasionally stayed overnight. I didn't bother him and he didn't bother me. Much. Only when he was the reason breakfast wasn't served on time because he and The Girlfriend were too busy giggling in the bedroom. Then I minded a lot and had to scratch the door to get their attention.

Since The Girlfriend and I weren't that close, I didn't mind not sharing her bed, especially not when her man was around.

I slept in a corner of the living room in my blue doggie bed that matched the colour of the curtains. Apparently that was very important, judging by the countless times The Girlfriend told other people about it.

On the whole I was more or less content. Apart from the times when I was made to wear whatever outfit matched The Girlfriend's current handbag. That was less great, but I humoured her because the food was still great and I still hadn't figured out what was nagging me inside.

Then, one day, when I had finally resigned myself to the fact that life was going to be very safe, but rather predictable and not very exciting, something peculiar happened.

The Girlfriend had taken me with her on her daily walk to the shops. It was the same routine as always and the day in question was no different from any other.

We stopped outside the bakery, The Girlfriend tied me to the railings and, without another word, turned to go inside, leaving me to my own devices. I spent the time contemplating how unfair it was that I could never get to any of the things inside that smelled so good.

For a while I just sat there, eyes closed, sniffing the warm air that was wafting over me from inside the shop, whenever the doors opened to let people in and out. There were yummy sweet smells and even yummier savoury smells, and everything in between.

I was trying my hardest not to drool on the pavement, when I suddenly saw her – a woman standing in the queue by the till inside the bakery.

I didn't recognise her, but there was something

strangely familiar about her nevertheless. I tried but couldn't place what it was, no matter how long and hard I stared at her. And then she spotted me too and made this weird and rather loud 'OHH' sound. As if she was in pain. Or… as if she had recognised me.

But I just couldn't remember if or where I knew her from. I just had this feeling that part of me wanted to run to her, and part of me wanted to tell her off for something.

And then the woman took her phone out of her bag and most annoyingly began to take pictures of me. I wasn't in the mood for that AT ALL, and so I turned away and gave her the cold shoulder.

The Girlfriend, who saw all this happening as she was standing in line to pay for her purchases, also got annoyed and flashed the woman a very dirty look. And another, even filthier one, when she was finally done and walked past her out of the shop to untie me.

It wasn't until I was roughly pulled down the street by The Girlfriend – even though I hadn't done anything – that I suddenly remembered… *something…*

A glimpse, no more:

… a huge sofa that felt awfully comfortable… the woman from the shop wiggling her finger at me… me snapping at once at said finger – because you NEVER, EVER wiggle your finger at me!!!… a voice shouting, 'Oh no, did he bite you?'… a voice that immediately

*made my heart pound and felt so very much like Home –
never mind that it also presently sounded rather peeved
with me... and...*

Nothing else.

But by that time we had already rounded the
corner and crossed the street, rounded yet another
corner, and walked to the end of that street as well.
And try as I might, I couldn't get another glimpse of
the woman from the shop. Nor could I remember
anything else.

I slept a lot after that, because in my dreams I
could *almost* remember and I could listen to the
beautiful music and pretend that I was *Home*.

What I didn't know at the time was that it had been
my Auntie Pachy that day who indeed thought she
had recognised me the very moment she had
spotted me outside the bakery. But because she
couldn't quite believe her eyes and wasn't *completely*
sure that it was really me – and also because The
Girlfriend kept shooting her filthy looks to put her
off, just in case she was one of those nasty people
who steal dogs – Auntie Pachy didn't approach The
Girlfriend to ask about me. She came to regret that
quite a lot later on, I can tell you!

But she did try to take my picture which, she later told my mum on the phone, had been almost impossible because I kept turning away from her. In the end she only got one half decent picture which she immediately sent to my mum and dad.

My parents couldn't believe what they were seeing, but they didn't want to get their hopes up, just in case the picture only showed a little dog that happened to look very similar to me.

My auntie however had no such doubts. She told my mum that she regretted very much that she had lost track of me during the time it took her to reach the till and pay for her purchases. She left the shop in a hurry after that, hoping to get another glimpse of me, but just couldn't. She was so certain that it had been me, that she told my mum she was going to go back to the bakery the next morning to try and see if she could find me again. Or at least talk to the sales assistant and find out if anyone knew who the woman who had been with me was, and where she lived.

Nice plan, but here is where life threw us all a nasty curveball – wouldn't it just?!!

When my rather excited auntie arrived at the bakery the very next day, she got a nasty shock, and simply couldn't believe what her eyes were telling her.

Because it had gone.

Completely.

Nothing at all was left of the bakery! Not even the doors. The entire shop that had been there for half a century, had gone overnight. All that was left of it was an empty, boarded-up shell. Auntie Pachy was so utterly incredulous she took a picture of it and sent it to my mum, who remembers the bakery well, and also couldn't believe what she was seeing.

And unfortunately that was that.

My auntie's plan to go to the bakery every day until she found me again, would have surely worked out because The Girlfriend was, as my aunt suspected, a creature of habit and would have gone back to where she bought her bread and pastries on a twice-weekly basis.

But now the bakery was gone, and Buenos Aires is a *HUUUUUUUUGE* city with thousands more bakeries than I have toes on my feet.

And so, even though Auntie Pachy combed the neighbourhood and all the other bakeries in the area during the weeks and months that followed, she had missed the tiny window of opportunity for finding me again.

She could have saved me a lot of heartache if she had, too.

But as it was she never saw me again.

Chapter 2

ANOTHER COUNTRY

As I was blissfully unaware of what was going on back home with my family in the UK, I put the whole episode of the lady in the bakery firmly out of my mind, and life went back to normal.

Until one morning, when mid-one-of-my-snoozes, all of a sudden The Girlfriend walks in, all smiles, with LOADS of bags in her hands. Bags that hadn't been there when she left a few hours ago.

For once she hadn't taken me along with her on her endless shopping spree because she felt bad about leaving her man behind at home and all alone. So she left me too. To keep him company. Not that either of us particularly appreciated the sentiment.

She dumped all her shopping bags, bar one, down on the living room floor, and then proceeded to pull out what had been hidden inside the one she was still clutching in her hand.

At first we couldn't tell whatever it was, because in her excitement she was waving it so frantically around in the air that all we could see was a blur of arm and… something. Luckily she didn't do it for long because it was seriously making me dizzy. At last she stopped her frantic waving-about and presented to us what she was holding in her hand with a dramatic flourish and proudly proclaimed, 'SORPREEEEEEEESAAAAA!!!'.

Loudly. And in a *very* shrill voice, which made me flinch and her man wince.

Well, let me tell you, it wasn't really such a surprise, even though she said so. Because when her man and I both looked up at what she was dangling in front of our faces, we realised it was only *yet another* handbag. Okay, so it was bigger *and* matched the colour of a smaller one she had purchased only a few days ago, but other than that it was just… well, a bag. But boy, was she excited about it! Her man was decidedly less excited, judging by the fake grin on his face. I personally couldn't have cared less, but then The Girlfriend grabbed me in – what I thought – was a rare show of affection, until she proceeded to stuff me inside the new bag. I wasn't best pleased about it, I can tell you!! But then I mulled things over and decided to let her – I figured it would earn me a treat or two.

Not that it did.

The Girlfriend spent quite some time yabbering away merrily about this and that whilst I was stuck inside the new bag, waiting in vain for my treat. I caught her saying something about a 'trip of a lifetime' and 'we can take him, my aunt does the same with hers all the time' and 'come on, it'll be fun'. Then something about '*amazing* shopping in Miami' which immediately made me feel bored and sleepy and had just about the same effect on her man, from what I could tell.

Still no treat…

By the time The Girlfriend had talked her man around and into whatever her plans were, I realised no treats would be forthcoming and so I quit the stupid bag I was sitting in. I mean, what do you take me for?!! I'm not a toy!!!

Unfortunately for me that wasn't the end of the whole sorry episode. Starting the very next day, what followed were a string of COMPLETELY UNNECESSARY trips to the vet's and lots of needles and injections. And slowly, bit by bit, I started to remember the intense dislike I had had for the profession during my past life. Luckily for the vet, by the time he was finally done with whatever he was subjecting me to, and after he handed what he called a *pet passport* to The Girlfriend, we took our leave and I never, ever saw him again.

Good riddance is all I can say!

What do I remember of the flight to Miami? Not much. I was heavily sedated – my parting gift from the vet. I sat inside the accursed bag for hours!! Completely whacked. Didn't care about a thing. Couldn't eat. Didn't even pee or poo. Or if I did I don't remember.

The dangerous thing with memories is that you can't choose what you remember, or when. But after that last visit to the vet's, on the way to the airport, I suddenly remembered my Rule Number One – DON'T TOUCH MY BOTTOM! OR MY BACK! from my former life. Despite being drugged. I didn't remember how, why or when I'd come up with it, but I remembered having enforced it rigorously in the past by first flashing my teeth and then – should that warning be ignored by whoever was foolish enough to break said rule – following up with a well-earned nip. As soon as I remembered that one, it felt completely right and natural to implement the rule once more, there and then and from now on.

Unfortunately that was a memory that almost got me killed a little while later on. You'll see what I mean when I tell you what happened.

I decided to make an exception to the rule for The Girlfriend. Because she provided the food. Even though she'd taken me to the vet's and stuffed me inside the stupid bag I was currently residing in. But one has to be practical given the circumstances.

Her man however was a different matter. Especially since deep down I hadn't forgiven him for the rude inspection he had subjected me to prior to making me a Christmas present to his girlfriend. And I have a *loooong* memory.

He was rather surprised when I snarled at him when he stuck his finger into the bag and touched my back on the plane, I can tell you! The look on his face was priceless! Unfortunately I was far too groggy to follow through on my threat, but I guess he got the drift. Even though he put the whole episode down to my being drugged. I was rather looking forward to showing him that it had NOTHING AT ALL to do with the drugs, but due to what happened next I unfortunately never got the chance.

I was still groggy by the time The Girlfriend picked me up, inside the bag, and carried me off the airplane. I remember everything in a bit of a haze. Long corridors, waiting in line with LOADS of other people, the man picking up lots of suitcases, waiting in line again. And waiting some more. And being picked up, and put down, and picked up again. Like I was a bloody parcel.

The whole thing was also starting to make me seriously seasick. Which sparked another memory… *something about being on a boat… and not liking it one single bit…*

But as that memory was completely useless to me in the current situation, I let it go.

Then, FINALLY, we were outside. I still couldn't move much, but as I sniffed the air to get a feel of the place, I got the urge to get out of the bag and mark my territory. Couldn't do it though, so I made do with marking the inside of the bag. Well, okay, so I just let go – what did you expect me to do??? My legs were still not working properly, thanks to the vet's ministrations. The Girlfriend didn't notice as she put me down, still inside my bag, next to all the other luggage.

I looked up at her, expecting to finally be lifted out of the damn bag, but she was too busy looking around for her man and totally ignored me.

And that was the last time I saw her.

Ever.

Because while her attention was I-don't-know-where, someone else picked me up. Bag and all. He also picked two of The Girlfriend's other matching bags up at the same time. And then he hurried towards a waiting car, flung me and the other luggage unceremoniously inside, hopped in beside the driver – who I couldn't see properly from where I had landed – and off we went.

And just like that the part of my life that involved The Girlfriend and her man was over.

Now I don't know if you know this, but Miami is HUGE. Not as huge as Buenos Aires, but it still took us ages to get to where the two men in the car wanted to go. Since I still wasn't feeling completely myself, I only vaguely cared about the indignity of having to sit in my own pee for what seemed like hours. When the car finally stopped, guess where they took me? To a vet!!! As if I wasn't drugged enough already!!

This one looked – and smelled – decidedly shifty. He said something about a chip having to come out and needing to knock me out for the procedure.

Before I could object I already felt a needle going into my skin.

I mean, what is it with vets??!! Don't they have better things to do than to constantly stick needles into dogs' bottoms???

As it happens, I couldn't complete the thought before everything went black.

When I came to I wasn't inside the bag anymore. But before I could get all excited about that fact, I noticed that I was now in a cage. Inside a dark, musty smelling place. All by myself! Luckily, whoever had dumped me there had left me some food and water. The food was substandard and not at all what I'd been used to so far, but the water was great. And boy, was I thirsty! I gulped the whole content of the bowl down in one go. Of course it immediately made me want to pee, but I couldn't figure out how to get out of the stupid cage I was in. In the end I had to do my business in the corner of the cage. The Girlfriend would have had a fit if she'd seen it, but what could I do?

I also noticed that the back of my neck was smarting, but couldn't get to it to lick it better. Since I wasn't exactly sure what to do next, I decided to have a snooze. Must have slept for quite some time because, when I woke up, I finally felt so much more like myself again. And now I was HUNGRY. Could have eaten a horse! Well, not really, but you know what I mean.

And the more I thought about what had happened to me, I was also starting to feel more and more irate about the whole situation. So I decided to let rip at last. Did a few test barks first and then followed them up with a non-stop barking rant about the indignity of it all. At the top of my voice. Really got into it, too. I never really had been given much reason to bark during my life with The Girlfriend, and so I had forgotten just how good it felt to let the whole neighbourhood know when you're feeling thoroughly and utterly peeved about something.

Whilst I was carrying on like this, I had a vague memory of having barked like this before. But before I could dwell on the thought, the door to the musty place was flung open and, as he came running towards me, I recognised the man who had stolen me inside my bag at the airport. He was angry and smelled scared at the same time. And he was telling me in no uncertain terms to 'SHUT UP!'

But I wasn't having any of it. REALLY told him what I thought of him in ear-splitting, spittle-spraying, teeth-baring barks. Only calmed down when he picked up a baseball bat and started to clobber the top of my cage with it. Well, okay, it was more a case of cowering down as low as possible and shaking and whining quite a bit because no one had ever done something like that to me before.

That's when suddenly a second man emerged in the doorway. He smelt vaguely familiar and I reckon he was the one who had been driving the car when they took me to the vet's before. Now he was shouting at the first man, telling him to calm down and think of the money they wouldn't get if he pounded me to a pulp as he'd been threatening to just a minute ago. Then he suddenly opened the door to my cage and, as I was cringing away from whatever would happen next, he surprised me by clipping a lead to the new collar I hadn't even noticed I was now wearing. They must have exchanged it with my old one while I was out for the count, after my visit to the vet's.

The second man then used the lead to pull me out of the cage. As much as I hated the cage, I really wasn't sure about leaving it now either. Especially given the company I was currently in.

But as he didn't smell angry like the first man, and kept talking to me in low tones, telling me to 'Come on, be a good little doggie, come on out…', I decided to give it a go. Anything rather than risk being stuck with the first man. Just to be on the safe side, I made myself as small as possible when his hand came towards me. But he only adjusted my collar and put some weird smelling ointment on my neck. And I was smart enough to suspend Rule Number One for the time being.

Then he told me that I was a good boy and coaxed me to come with him. So we walked out through the door together and into a dirty looking yard. Shouting back over his shoulder, he told the first man to clean the cage and fetch me some food and water. Not sure the first man wanted to, judging from the smell he was emitting, but I reckon, like myself, he didn't have a choice in the matter.

We walked around in circles for a while and I got the drift that the man wanted me to pee and poo. So I obliged. This earned me more praise and then it was back inside, which I *really* didn't want to do, but did anyway. I figured, pick your fights when you can win them. At least the cage was clean now, and I could see that the two bowls the first man had placed inside contained enough food and water to keep me going. Since I didn't want him to give me a repeat performance with the baseball bat, I decided to pretend to be on my best behaviour. At least until I had figured out a way to escape.

I spent the whole night worrying inside my cage. The very next day, both men were back. This time they both smelled excited and happy which is why I didn't need any coaxing to leave the cage. I ran past the first man, careful not to growl or flash my teeth at him, even though I really wanted to, because NOTHING WAS FORGOTTEN OR FORGIVEN, and followed the second man out into the dirty yard.

I did my business, wondering what would happen next, when the first man grabbed me roughly from behind and wrapped me up inside a blanket. Now, as you know, this was the second time someone had done that to me and I was getting rather fed up with it all. Still, I also remembered that the man had a temper, and the baseball bat wasn't far away, so I froze and let him carry me for now. I was busy contemplating my options when I noticed that he had carried me outside and to the car I'd been inside before.

However, since I wasn't sedated any longer, he took no chances and quickly dumped me into the boot of the car and banged it shut before I could object. I did quite a bit of snarling as the car drove off, I can tell you!

But I also made sure to shut up again when the boot was opened once more.

Luckily it was the second man. He lifted me out of the boot and told me to be a good boy, and to make sure that I was on my best behaviour. And since I didn't want to find out what would happen if

I didn't comply, I played along. For now.

The first man was told to stay in the car, which was great because I was in no hurry to see him again.

We crossed the road and walked along a leafy, green path together, past a row of white houses with lots of trees on either side. I was trying to decide which one to mark first, but before I even had the chance to cock my leg, I was pulled towards one of the houses.

The man rang the doorbell, and after a short while a young woman with long hair and a young man with glasses opened the door. They didn't look like they would be a match for the man I was with, and especially not for the other one waiting in the car, but for now the second man was on his best behaviour. I suddenly noticed that he had changed his clothes and shoes for the occasion. They smelled new and clean, not like the ones he had worn before. He also now sported glasses. Dark ones, so you couldn't see his eyes.

'Oh hi!', I heard him say. And even his voice sounded different. Friendlier. Make that sickly sweet. Whilst smelling of sweat and excitement.

'I'm Dan. We spoke earlier on the phone. You must be Jessica and Joshua.'

Now, you can bet your bottom dollar that his name wasn't 'Dan', that's for sure! But I was intrigued as to why he was going to such lengths to cosy up to the new people, so I sat down on the doorstep next to him.

Spotting me, Jessica immediately squatted down and *awwww*ed at me at length. And then she stroked my head. First with one, and then with both hands. Luckily for her that was all she stroked. Mind you, knowing that the first man was still waiting in the car, I would have probably let her stroke every inch of me. Just in case he had brought his baseball bat along.

'This is Trigger', I heard the man say. I almost did a double take. I sure as hell had never been called Trigger before. Benito, the name The Girlfriend had bestowed on me, of course hadn't been my real name either, but at least it wasn't a stupid name like Trigger!

'Hey Trigger! *Awww*…. You're so cute!', Jessica crooned. And then Joshua also crouched down by her side to awkwardly ruffle the hair on top of my head. I still wasn't sure where any of this was going, but I was very much enjoying the attention, when I suddenly heard the man by my side say, 'We live just over there', pointing vaguely somewhere into the distance. Which of course was a complete and utter lie. And not just because he smelled all wrong when he said it. Judging from the long trip in the car we had just made, he lived miles away. In the wrong direction. And it sure wasn't lovely and friendly either. It was filthy and dark like the cage I had been in.

'It's such a lovely, safe and friendly neighbourhood, don't you think?'

The young couple agreed, but they were a bit distracted stroking me, and must have missed the lie. They both straightened up when the man said, 'Anyhow, it's such a shame we have to give him away. He's such a great little dog, but, like I told you, unfortunately my wife is very sick and with the new baby on the way, and…' Yadi-yadi-ya!

At this stage I zoned out. Too many lies, not much point listening, and a rather yummy smell distractingly wafting at me from inside the house. Smelling *soooo* much nicer than the food I'd had to make do with lately. So, I started to drool. Left a right little puddle of drool right there on the pavement. Couldn't help myself. Also, it had been a while since I'd last eaten. And then my tummy growled loudly to emphasize the point.

At that, Jessica giggled and looked at Joshua, who looked back at her and nodded. And then they faced the man, mind made up. 'We'll take him', Joshua said. At this, the man positively beamed and flashed them as smile so wide that all his teeth were showing. 'Are you sure?', he asked them. Not sure how anyone could have missed the false tone AND the smell, but hey, that's humans for you. When he added, 'Oh, my wife and I will miss him so much!', I was almost sick on the doormat. I mean, really!!! As far as I knew he didn't even have a wife. Just a mean friend with a baseball bat who stole little dogs who were marooned inside poncy travel bags at stupid airports.

'I'm so sorry', Jessica replied, and 'We promise to look after him.' At that Joshua handed over an envelope to the man.

And that's when I understood what was going on here.

I was being sold again. Only difference being that this time I wasn't a Christmas present.

Things progressed rather fast after that. My lead changed hands, I was pulled inside Jessica and Joshua's house – not that I needed much pulling – and I didn't even look back as the door closed behind me. The man in his eagerness hadn't even pretended to say goodbye to his beloved 'Trigger'. And I was glad to have seen the last of him and his unsavoury friend. So I quickly strutted down the corridor, pulling Jessica along, Joshua in tow, straight into the kitchen. Just followed the smell really. Simple as. Then stared at them. Pointedly. Until some food was finally forthcoming. Didn't take her and Joshua all that long to figure it out, even though I could tell that they had never had a dog before.

And just like that I had a home again.

It wasn't my *Home*, the one I had begun to suspect was somewhere out there. But it was a place to rest and plan, and hopefully remember whatever it was I had forgotten.

Chapter 3

A NEW LIFE

Jessica and Joshua's house was much bigger than The Girlfriend's apartment had been, but unfortunately it didn't have much comfy furniture in it, as I soon discovered – apart from a sofa in the living room and a large bed with tons of cushions on it in the bedroom. I was grateful they had gone to such lengths to make me feel at home – until they told me off for getting up on the bed. That *really* confused me. Had I missed something? Was there a particular time for snoozing only? It didn't make any sense. Still, I was so glad that I wasn't with the two men who had stolen me any longer that I decided to humour them for now.

Not for long though.

After the hiccup with the bed, Jessica and Joshua showed me around some more. Well okay, I explored, and they followed. Jessica giggled a lot, and kept repeating 'Oh look, Josh, isn't he just the cutest?'. I was too busy checking the place out, so I didn't turn around, but I could hear that there was a lot of kissing and hugging going on behind me.

One of the things Jessica and Joshua proudly pointed out to me was a brand-new doggie bed they had placed in the corner of the living room, right by the huge glass doors through which I could see the back garden. I wasn't all that interested in the doggie bed as I was already looking forward to sleeping on the big bed. So I ignored it. Didn't even try it out for size.

But I did like the back garden behind the huge glass doors, Jessica and Joshua eventually opened for me so I could explore. It wasn't very big but had some grassy spots with stone tiles all around them and lots of bushes on either side. Oh, and fancy furniture that was way too hard and uncomfortable to sit on. Trust me, I tried and it wasn't a great experience.

There were also LOADS of pots with plants in them. Not sure why they needed pots, but I quickly marked them anyway, just to make sure any passing cats would know that this house and its garden were now taken.

I could tell that Jessica wasn't too happy about it because I heard her say 'Oh no!' a few times in rapid succession. But she also understood that I needed to pee somewhere, so she told Joshua that it might be a better idea to take me to the park instead of letting me use the back garden as a bathroom. Fine by me – I liked parks better anyhow.

When I was done exploring the house and garden, I lay down on the rug by the sofa and snoozed for a while. I woke up because I felt Jessica and Joshua staring at me. I could tell from the way they were watching me that they couldn't have seen many dogs sleep. Not close up anyhow.

As soon as I opened my eyes, Jessica stroked my back, but when I swivelled around, wondering if now was a good time to introduce her to Rule Number One, she quickly snatched her hand away and talked to me instead. 'Hey Trigger, wanna go for a walk?' I decided I did – never mind the 'Trigger'.

Outside was very different from where I had lived before. Wide, long streets, and not so many houses. And loads of trees for marking. I made the most of it, but we didn't walk very far that first day because Jessica and Joshua seemed keen to get back home. But I briefly got to see the park a few blocks down from their house. It was very green, with even more trees and bushes, and it also had a playground for children in it. That's what Jessica explained to me anyhow when I tried to pull closer to explore the colourful strange metal frames and structures. I really wanted to mark everything in sight, but Joshua, who was holding my lead at the time, wouldn't let me. Apparently it was off limits to dogs. I promised myself we'd see about that one as soon as I was off the lead.

Back at the house, I marched back into the kitchen, even though my lead was still attached, to let Jessica and Joshua know that it was dinnertime. Just in case they hadn't realised. I have to say they were very obliging. And the food was acceptable. Not as good as The Girlfriend's had been, but as there was no way I could tell them about it, I made do.

They talked to me a lot that day. Babytalk mainly. And I just stared at them and let them get on with it. Even let them stroke my head.

The only thing that went massively pear-shaped in the evening were the sleeping arrangements. Jessica and Joshua must have misunderstood my intentions with regards to the use of the new doggie bed. As in – I was NOT going to use it. I WAS going to use the big bed with the many cushions.

Turns out, they didn't get it.

The whole debacle began right after Jessica and Joshua had had their own dinner – of which I didn't get a titbit even though I begged for it. Repeatedly! Had to wait until they got up from the table and then jump up on the chair and help myself. Promised myself there and then that I had to teach them better.

Anyway, dinner over and done with, Jessica and Joshua decided to watch some telly. Not very exciting, but as I was still tired from all the events of the day, I snoozed some more on the living room rug. You may be wondering, why not on the sofa? Well, it was a leather sofa and looked slippery. Which is why I chose to lie on the rug that was furry and warm instead. Also, I was getting colder by the minute because, like The Girlfriend, Jessica and Joshua had a big box in the house that kept blowing cold air into my face. I much preferred the hot temperature outside in the garden and the park, but the stupid box was way too far up the wall for me to try and get to it to make it stop.

When Jessica and Joshua were done watching telly, they took me for one last walk around the block and then told me, 'Time for bed, Trigger!' How I hated that name! But I was also looking forward to sleeping some more. So I ran into the bedroom, jumped right up onto the bed, made myself a nest among the many cushions and waited for Jessica and Joshua to catch up with me.

Problem was, they seemed to have other ideas. Kept calling me over to the living room and showing me the doggie bed. But of course I wasn't having any of it. And no amount of pointing at it and telling me to get in was going to do the trick. No way!! I simply turned around, went straight back to the big comfy bed and then pointedly ignored their pleading and cajoling. And of course Jessica and Joshua were far too timid to make me move by force, and they knew it. And so did I.

Unfortunately they then tricked me. Waved a super tasty treat right in my face, but just far away enough so I couldn't get to it. And of course that turned out to be too big a temptation for me. Followed it right out of the bedroom and only realised I had been conned when the bedroom door closed behind me with Jessica and Joshua on one side and me on the other. The wrong side, as you might have guessed by now. Bloody cheek!

After a fair amount of scratching at the door, I decided to let it go. Lay down on the rug once more – no way was I EVER going to use the doggie bed after that – and made plenty of plans how to proceed the next morning.

I have to say, it didn't take me very long after that to teach Jessica and Joshua what I wanted from life. After all that had happened to me, sometime during that first night on the rug at their place, I promised myself not to follow anyone else's rules anymore. Figured it hadn't gotten me very far to do so, and seeing that Jessica and Joshua were rather inexperienced when it came to dogs, I decided to put down some rules of my own instead. Oh, and to ignore theirs whenever they came up with any. Which wasn't often, but tended to be rather annoying when it happened. But I learned quite quickly that nothing much would happen whenever I chose to ignore their rules, since they weren't exactly the baseball-bat-swinging type. As soon as I had figured that one out, I henceforth ignored *all* their rules and, in no time at all, they had learned that dogs are in charge.

Always.

At first they didn't mind so much and found the whole thing charming and funny. At least that's what I heard Jessica tell her friend on the phone.

On the first day after my arrival, as soon as Jessica and Joshua went to work and left me to my own devices, I used the opportunity to make myself right at home and finally mark my territory properly at last. They didn't find this all that charming and funny when they popped in to check on me around lunchtime that day.

I did get put outside into the garden for a while afterwards and told to 'Never do *that* again!'

After an hour or so in the garden, I came to agree with them. Reluctantly.

But I was adamant that all my other rules would stay in place. Especially the one about the big bed really being mine.

As soon as Jessica and Joshua had gone back to work once more, I raced to the bedroom, nudged the door they had conveniently forgotten to close properly, open with my nose and then spent endless hours pulling the big duvet into the right shape and building a safe haven for myself out of the many pillows. After I had ripped the filling out of the covers it became so much easier to shape them just the way I wanted to.

Jessica and Joshua found that even less charming and funny when they came home that evening. Unfortunately, after that I got put into the laundry room whenever they weren't home. They would use my lead to pull me there because they knew full well that I wouldn't have gone in otherwise. And even more unfortunately, they also put me there during the night. With the new doggie bed I didn't want to use. So I wouldn't scratch the bedroom door to demand entry whenever they went to bed.

The first time they put me in the laundry room, I managed to open the door and go back to MY bed. But regrettably after that, they made sure to always lock the laundry room door, so no amount of scratching and bashing the door handle would open it.

I was very bored and not exactly pleased to see them when they got home in the evening. I mean, how would you like it if you were locked in a small room for hours on end? With nothing to do but stare at the washing machine and the tumble drier? I sure wasn't in the mood for cuddles after that.

But I did allow them to take me for walks.

Like I told you, the neighbourhood was great, with plenty of trees for sniffing and marking. I also really liked the park because I could run around at last and have some fun. Sometimes alone and sometimes with other dogs, who were way more friendly than the ones I had encountered back with The Girlfriend.

At first Jessica and Joshua didn't let me off the lead, but then one day we met this old man in the park who told them to give it a try. I immediately liked him a lot because you could just tell that he really loved and understood dogs. And all the dogs in the park loved him right back. He really seemed to get us, and always had loads of treats for us. So, we in turn made sure to run to him every time he called us over. He remembered all our names, too. Even my wrong one. But I forgave him for using it – figured it was really Jessica and Joshua's fault for giving it to him.

I made the most of my outings to the park because back home wasn't exactly exciting. Jessica and Joshua worked long hours, and when they came home at last all they wanted to do was sit on the sofa, watch the telly and relax. But I was already relaxed from the endless hours in the boring laundry room with nothing to do. And I wanted to do stuff and play. But since they didn't comply, I did the only thing I could – I went back to snoozing for hours on end, listening to the music inside my head, trying to remember. But try as I might I still couldn't remember my former life.

Like I said, I didn't remember my real name either until one day a curious thing happened in the park. Joshua had taken me there on one of the rare days he was off work during the day. He was sitting on a bench, watching me play 'fetch that stick, but don't bring it back' with a little boy who happened to be quite acceptable as far as little boys go, and who seemed to have taken an instant shine to me. I didn't even have to nip him to keep him from touching my back and bottom.

As I was running around, finding sticks, hiding sticks, peeing on sticks – to stop anyone else from ever picking them up again – then rolling over and over in the mud and grass under the trees, leaves swirling madly wherever I went, I suddenly heard a woman shout, 'NELSON!', and then again, louder and more insistent this time, '*NEEEELSOOON!*'

And that's when something deep inside myself went very, very still.

But my feet... my feet had started to run. Straight towards that sound.

The little boy was also running. He got there first and the woman scooped him up into her arms and whirled him around and around, chanting 'There you are! There you *a... a... are!*' in that weird singsong-baby-talk voice grown-up humans use with their kids.

I looked up at her, and she looked down at me, and I realised that I didn't know her after all. She didn't know me either judging by the puzzled look on her face. But as I was trying to figure out what had made me run over to her in the first place, I heard her say 'It's alright, Nelson, the doggie is just saying hello.'

And that's when something clicked into place inside my head.

And I remembered my name.

I sat down with this buzzing sound inside my head, trying to make sense of it all. I knew for sure now that my name was Nelson, but even though I tried really hard, I couldn't remember anything else. I kept mulling it over and over in my head, all the way back home from the park and right through dinner, but nothing else was forthcoming.

Unfortunately, after that it became rather hard for Jessica and Joshua because from that moment on and with immediate effect I refused to react to the name they were calling me. I mean, wouldn't you??!! If you knew your name is Nelson why would you react to being called Trigger? Stupid name, anyhow!

Problem was, they didn't get why I was doing

this. And I knew they didn't speak enough dog to understand, so I didn't even bother trying to explain.

In the end they came to the conclusion that I was either becoming even more difficult all of a sudden and for no apparent reason at all, or that I was possibly going deaf. Since I had been *mainly* easy-going in that respect up to that point, they decided it must be the latter. Which is why they took me to the vet's to check out my ears – can you believe it?!!!

But of course the vet couldn't find anything wrong with my ears, and so he suggested they take me to doggie classes for some behaviour training instead. Trust a vet to come up with a silly idea like that!

But silly or not, take me to doggie classes they did. Unfortunately for Jessica and Joshua though it didn't make the slightest bit of a difference as there was nothing wrong with my behaviour in the first place. At least not in my book. I simply didn't want to be called by the wrong name any longer.

What followed was a rather frustrating time for all of us. They kept calling me Trigger, and I kept ignoring them whenever they did. I would still react when they told me to 'Sit!' and 'Come here!' – well, ok, *most* of the time, and of course only when a treat was in the offing. But whenever they used the wrong name to make me do things I simply refused point blank to do them.

So then it was stalemate.

Also, as this argument went on and on and things were becoming more and more frustrating for both sides, deep down I was more and more sure that it wasn't just my name that was wrong. I mean, things were still sort of acceptable when I was awake and running around in the park, doing my own stuff. But whenever I was locked inside the laundry room, or when I was just about to drop off to sleep, I got this distinct feeling that I was also in the wrong place, and that *Home* was somewhere else completely. It nagged and nagged at me and I simply couldn't shake it.

And then there were the dreams. Since I spent so much time snoozing, I had more and more of them. I could never remember them completely, but there were glimpses of things that made me feel all warm inside. Little things, like someone nibbling my ear, and I just *knew* it wasn't a dog. And pebbles being thrown just for me, and the smell of salt in the air. And always, always the sound of music all around me. I couldn't help but sing along to it, but sadly it didn't sound quite the same when it came out of my mouth in a never-ending howl.

Which made Jessica and Joshua take me to the

52

vet's again.

Of course he still couldn't find anything wrong with me, but Jessica and Joshua were getting more and more fed up with the whole situation, until one day they finally decided they couldn't cope any longer with a little dog that only followed his own rules, didn't answer to his name and howled all night long.

And that's how I ended up in a shelter.

I didn't know at first that's what the strange place with the concrete floors and the doggie smells all over was, as I walked in with Jessica and Joshua. They had taken me there right after – what I didn't realise at the time – was my last outing to the park. At first I was really excited that we were going somewhere I hadn't been to before, but I soon found out that it wasn't good news after all.

As soon as we arrived, we were met by a lady in a flowery dress who seemed very kind – judging by the size of the treat she gave me – and we all sat down for a chat. I wasn't allowed up on the colourful sofa, and so I sat down next to it and waited more or less patiently for whatever would happen next. I didn't really listen to what was being said, but after a little while the lady in the flowery dress got up and took us through another set of doors.

And guess who was waiting for us there?

Oh yes, ANOTHER vet!! Couldn't they tell that I was healthy and well?!! This one was a woman. She thoroughly checked me all over while I was forced to wear a muzzle – because I had dared to object to the unwarranted examination.

When she was done with all the poking and prodding, she looked through some papers Jessica and Joshua presented to her. She must have liked what she saw because she told the lady in the flowery dress that all was in order. I was mightily glad to hear her say that, too, because it meant she wasn't going to stick any needles into my bottom.

I was now more than ready to go back home and have my well-deserved dinner. But we only walked back into the reception room and Jessica and Joshua sat down once more for yet *another* chat with the lady in the flowery dress.

Then, all of a sudden, they both got up. I got up, too, but they told me to 'Sit!' and 'Stay!' and I complied because they hadn't called me Trigger.

And then they walked out of the door. I didn't try to follow. Just sat there and stared at the closing door.

And I never, ever saw them again.

It was the weirdest thing. But somehow it also seemed strangely familiar. As if this hadn't been the first time something like this had happened to me. But it was only a feeling as I still didn't remember anything else.

Chapter 4

THE SHELTER

The name shelter implies that it shelters you. Only this one didn't do that at all. Not really. It was horrible.

Let me explain.

A minute or so after Jessica and Joshua had left, the woman in the flowery dress got up and told me to follow her. I was curious as to what would happen next, so I did. Even though she called me Trigger.

We walked out through the door at the back of the room and down a staircase. And immediately things didn't look quite so friendly anymore. No more flowers on desks and colourful furniture to sit on. Only a long, grey corridor, with cages to the left, and cages to the right. All occupied by dogs of all shapes and sizes. *Soooo* many cages. And *soooooo* many dogs!

Some cages housed more than one dog, but most didn't. There was a lot of frantic barking going on – angry and nervous, desperate and bored, friendly and scared, and everything in between. And some dogs were cowering and didn't bother to bark at all.

I didn't answer back, but I also didn't really like being barked at, so I briskly followed the lady in the flowery dress down the corridor as quickly as I could. I figured she would take me out of the door at the other end of the corridor and somewhere nice.

I figured WRONG!

We were halfway down the corridor when the woman suddenly stopped. She wrote something on a white board next to one of the cages on the left. Then she opened the door of the cage and led me inside. I was puzzled. If I hadn't been, chances are I wouldn't have let her pull me inside. But as it was, I just stared at her, waiting for whatever would happen next.

She unclipped my lead, patted my head and told me, 'Good boy! Good job!' which was weird because I hadn't done anything. But hey, that's humans for you. Then she turned around, closed the door to the cage behind her, scribbled some more on the white board next to my cage, and simply walked away. Back to where we had come from.

I was stunned.

And then I joined in the barking. AT THE TOP OF MY VOICE!

And let me tell you, mine went from incredulous to almightily annoyed in less than two seconds flat! Did it for quite some time, too. Only, no one bothered to check on me.

I almost wished I was back with the two men who had stolen me at the airport. Even though one of them had wielded a baseball bat. But at least they had answered my barking.

I wished even more I was back with The Girlfriend. Even though life with her had been boring. But at least I had had my own apartment. And the food had been good. I was salivating just thinking about it.

But no amount of wishing brought any of them back.

And no, I didn't bother to wish for Jessica and Joshua. I hadn't forgotten that they had landed me in this mess in the first place.

After a while I finally shut up and decided to check out my cage. Someone had left a doggie bed in one corner. There was also some water in a bowl. And some dried food, which I first sniffed at, but then ate a few hours later. Beggars can't be choosers, as my mum would have said.

Then I decided to lay down in the doggie bed for a while, because there was nothing else to do.

Sometime later I heard the door at the end of the corridor open and voices talking to each other. This triggered the pandemonium of barking from almost every dog all over again. From where I was, I couldn't see the people until they walked right up to my cage.

And that's when I first met Sam.

I know this was his name because he introduced himself as soon as he opened the door to my cage. You see, that's the funny thing with humans – they either tell you immediately what they are called, or never. Which is highly annoying because then you have to guess.

If you can be bothered, that is.

Sam was of the first variety. He immediately crouched down to my level, let me sniff his outstretched hand, and said 'Hey Trigger, I'm Sam.' Now, there was no way to tell him that Trigger wasn't my real name and I didn't want to waste any time growling at him because he smelled just so friendly and *right*. In fact he reminded me of someone, but I just couldn't remember who. I instantly liked Sam. And I think he liked me too. So, I suspended Rule Number One. But only for him. For anyone else it still applied. And in time I enforced it vigorously.

Not long after that of course, I came to wish that I had never remembered the rule even existed because – as I told you before – it almost got me killed.

Sam spent quite some time stroking me all over, and I returned the favour by giving his face and hands a good, thorough wash with my tongue. It made him laugh and stroke me more, which was exceedingly nice after what I had just been through. Also, apart from the people in my dreams, no one had ever bothered to stroke me quite as much. I simply *loooooooved* it! Couldn't get enough of it.

When Sam finally got up and clipped my lead on, I fully expected him to take me home with him. But to my utter surprise he didn't. He took me out of my cage though. For a little while. Some of the other dogs got taken out as well by the other people who had come in with Sam. As they were talking to each other I picked up their names as well. There was Shania, Jamal, Brianna, Isabella, Ruben, Alicia,

Ashley, Julio and Sofia. Over time I got to meet them all, but although they all seemed kind of nice, deep down I much preferred Sam. By miles!

That day they took us out into the yard for a walk. I didn't bother saying hello to the other dogs because I still assumed Sam was going to take me home in a moment.

But as we were walking around and around and around in circles it slowly began to dawn on me that that wasn't going to happen. And just as I realised it, we were all taken back to our respective cages.

Sam changed my water and filled my food bowl. But then he left. And it sure was lonely after he had gone.

I really didn't understand why he hadn't taken me home. I was so sure he liked me an awful lot. And I had suspended Rule Number One just for him and not nipped or growled at him at all.

I simply couldn't figure out what had gone wrong.

I spent a long, lonely night all by myself in my cage. Thinking that this was even worse than the laundry room I had been locked in at Jessica and Joshua's. Didn't get much sleep that night, I was so worried.

But the morning after my first night at the shelter, Sam miraculously came back. I was so happy to see him I ran around like mad, and jumped up at him. Licked his hand like crazy, too. *And* his face – as soon as he crouched down and I could get to it.

I was just *soooooo* relieved that he had changed his mind, and kept barking at him to 'Hurry up already and take me home!'

I was so happy, I just couldn't sit still. Sam looked at me and laughed, and sure enough, he clipped my lead on and led me outside.

This time it was only me and Sam out in the yard. He unclipped my lead, picked up a ball and threw it for me. He told me to 'Fetch!' and I obliged and ran for it. But deep down I didn't understand why he would waste any time with playing. Surely we could play at length as soon as we got home.

So I carried the ball to the gate at the back of the yard, hoping he would get the drift and open it already, so we could leave together.

When he didn't oblige, I scratched at the door with both paws to make him understand. Weirdly, this seemed to make him sad. So I stopped and looked at him. He came over to me and for a longish while he only stroked my head. Then he told me to give him the ball, and after a quick wrestle I did. Anything to make Sam happy, so we could finally be on our way.

Only… that didn't happen.

Sam threw the ball a few more times for me, and I ran and picked it up half-heartedly and let him wrestle it out of my mouth.

But never once did he walk up to the gate to open it.

Not even when I sat down next to it and refused to play ball any longer. No, he just walked over to where I was sitting, stroked my head some more, clipped my lead back on and took me back to my cage. I tried to pull away from the door but he was stronger than I.

I still didn't think of nipping him or anything like that because he smelled almost as sad as I felt inside. He didn't leave immediately either.

For a very long time Sam sat on the floor beside me. He stroked me all over and told me how sorry he was. That's all he said. 'I'm sorry, Trigger. I'm sorry.' Over and over again.

Then he finally got up and left. I didn't try to run after him. Felt utterly rejected and REALLY didn't understand why he didn't want me even though I could tell that he liked me so much. Also *really* hated that I couldn't tell him that my name WASN'T BLOODY TRIGGER!!!

Later that day, the girl that was called Sofia came by to change my water and give me some food. It tasted exactly the same as the day before and was very dry, but I ate it all because I was hungry. Sofia tried her best to make friends with me, but I wasn't really in the mood and ignored her. Quickly flashed my teeth at her when she tried to stroke me. Didn't want to be touched and made sure she got it. She totally did, which is why she asked Ruben to take me for a walk when it was time to do so.

I was miserable, but I also needed to pee and poo and didn't want to do it inside my cage. So I let Ruben take me outside. He didn't spend any time playing, which was fine by me. Wasn't in the mood for it anyway.

Then it was back to my cage, and I was finally beginning to spot the pattern of life inside the shelter.

But the next day there was no Sam.

I felt more miserable than ever. This time it was Shania who changed my water and fed me. I couldn't have cared less. Luckily for her she also left me in peace. Well, ok, so I did have to warn her off before she did. But she got it pretty quickly. And once again it was Ruben who had to take me for my walk. I soon learned that he wasn't scared of any dog, which is why he was always called for whenever one of us was in a difficult mood. I wasn't the only one he walked that day either. Quite a lot of the other dogs had had quite enough of being cooped up in this place for no good reason at all.

After my walk I got fed again. And then it was back to counting the hours again, until someone else would show up.

After another long night contemplating the state of affairs, and not getting much sleep because the other dogs just wouldn't settle that night, I was bone tired, when I finally heard people coming in once more.

I wasn't really that interested any longer. But when my cage door was opened, it was Sam who stood in the doorway. And I simply couldn't be cross with him. Just couldn't help myself. Yapped a lot like a puppy, and jumped up and licked him all over. And was just so very, *very* happy to see him again.

We walked, we played, we cuddled A LOT, and most of all we pretended that everything was fine.

And then Sam left again. And I was left behind

once more, waiting and hoping he would come back and change his mind about taking me home.

The next day Sam came back early in the morning. He smelled a mixture of apprehensive, excited and happy to see me. And then he told me that someone had come to see me, and to make sure I was on my best behaviour. I didn't quite understand, but no matter how badly I wanted to leave this place, I rather hoped it wasn't Jessica and Joshua who had come back to get me.

Turns out it wasn't.

When Sam led me back to the room I had last seen Jessica and Joshua in, I was surprised to see a very large, smiling lady who I had never met before. Not sure why, but apparently she had come to see me together with her young son, who was very round and had a huge grin on his face. Unfortunately, it soon became apparent that the boy was also rather excitable and seemed to be overly fond of my tail. So, of course, I had to introduce him to Rule Number One at once.

As soon as he tried to make a grab for my tail, I forestalled him by barking 'DON'T TOUCH MY BOTTOM! OR MY BACK!!!' at the top of my voice.

This startled him so much that he fell backwards and landed heavily on his bottom. And then he started to bawl. Loudly. And to scramble away from me as fast as his chubby limbs allowed. His mum hurried over to him and snatched him up into her arms as fast as she could, which was no mean feat because her son *was* a rather hefty young chap.

Then they both left. In a hurry. At once.

I really thought Sam would approve, but for some strange reason he didn't. He told me off instead. I was quite shocked when he did. He didn't do it at length, but he didn't cuddle me either for some time afterwards. I tried to lick his hand as he walked me back to my cage but he wasn't having any of it.

The next day someone else came to see me. Actually, two different couples. One after the other. And that's when I finally understood what was going on. I was being inspected as a prospective Christmas present once more. Not that it was anywhere near Christmas. Not sure how I knew this, but I had this flash of a vivid memory at the thought... *A tree, covered in baubles and all sorts of other dangly bits. And a white plastic deer under it that meant...* something...

or should *have. And it was cold. Not at all like the Christmas when I had been presented to The Girlfriend by her man…*

The memory was so strong it made me shake my head. When I could get my bearings again, still standing in front of the first couple that had come to see me that day, I just knew that they were not my people. No matter how much they cooed and waved their treats at me.

And so I ignored them. Sidestepped each time they approached me, backed away as far from them as my lead allowed, and flashed my teeth when they still didn't get the hint.

The lady in the flowery dress was also in the room with Sam and the couple, and I heard her apologise to them, saying something about me needing further training. I needed no such thing! I just didn't want to end up with the wrong people again.

Also, there *was* a part of me that still hoped that Sam, seeing that I liked him best, would reconsider and finally take me home with him.

But he didn't. Not even after the visit of the second couple. Now, *they* didn't take the hint at all.

Had to snap and snarl at them when they ignored Rule Number One. Twice!!

After the last couple had left, the lady in the flowery dress told Sam to spend some time training me properly. How silly of her! Because OF COURSE I would have done anything for him.

Sam told me to 'Sit!' and – 'Trigger' or no 'Trigger' – I would sit. The same with 'Down!' and 'Come here!' and 'Fetch!' – okay, not so much that one, because where's the point in that??!! So much more fun grabbing the ball and having Sam wrestle it out of my mouth. And of course NOT ONCE did I snarl at him or flash my teeth. As I told you before, I really liked Sam a lot, and Rule Number One was permanently suspended when it came to him.

Only, the lady in the flowery dress didn't understand. The next time someone came to see me and I nipped them for touching my bottom, she shouted at Sam. 'Didn't you tell me he had changed?' and 'You know we can't rehome him if he still behaves like that!' And then Sam was apologising a lot, telling her I was really well behaved with him. But of course she didn't believe him. She told Sam something about having one more week 'or else...', but I wasn't really listening any longer.

All that counted was that I was happy being with Sam whenever I could. I didn't want another family anyway if I couldn't live with him. And surely, sooner or later, he would see sense and take me home with him at last.

But sadly I didn't know then what I know now, and so the inevitable happened.

Another week came and went. Sam didn't come to see me every day, but whenever he did, he 'trained' me.

Well, you can imagine how that one went.

On the days Sam wasn't around, more people came to visit me. And since nothing had changed from my perspective, nothing changed in the way I interacted with them. I mean, rules are rules. You don't touch my bottom or my back, I don't snarl. That's only fair. But of course not all of my visitors got that. Not my problem, as far as I was concerned.

Unfortunately I never knew what the consequences would be.

Chapter 5

ANOTHER GOODBYE

It was a wet and windy day. And it was a Wednesday. I knew this because Sam told Sofia so. Now, normally I don't really care what day it is, because I never quite understood why humans feel this strange need to give days names in the first place. It's not as if they could answer back when called. Also, if you *do* bother to name days it's kind of embarrassing to run out of names after the seventh, and then be lazy and start with name one again after that. Don't you think? Kind of pointless. And really confusing too. 'It's Wednesday.' Oh, yeah, which one is it? There seem to be quite a lot of them.

As I said, completely silly and pointless.

But on the day in question, when Sam told Sofia

'Oh, no, it's Wednesday!' with a voice laden with dread, something deep inside told me that a) this was bad news and b) that there was something about the word 'Wednesday' that I *should* remember.

But I didn't.

What I *did* know, however, was that whenever helpers at the shelter talked about that particular day, a cloud of doom seemed to descend on the place. There were no visitors that day either, but the woman who only came on that day would come down to the kennels and slowly make her way past kennel after kennel whilst everyone inside was trying to shrink into the shadows. And then she would stop at some kennel door or other and drag out whichever dog was in it. She would hurry down the long corridor with them, and out through the door none of us ever went through. Unless we were sick. Or were to be given pointless injections or pills. Or foul-smelling ointments behind the ears.

A few minutes later she would come back and repeat what she had been doing. Again. And again. And again.

We never knew where she took the dogs she took, but it sure wasn't for walkies. Because none of them ever came back.

And afterwards some of the helpers would always cry. I once saw a young girl cry so much she was sick in the corridor. That one never came back again afterwards.

And most of the other helpers wore the kind of

politely bland smile on their faces humans pull to make each other believe everything is just fine. Or when they don't want to talk about things. But of course they forget that we can smell the truth.

I guess that's the main difference between humans and dogs. When we are unhappy, we look *and* smell unhappy. But when humans are sad, their faces and voices can look and sound happy, but their whole body still smells sad. And that's really horrible because it twists them and does bad things to them inside. I never understood why they just don't let it all hang out. I ALWAYS did. So much easier to let everyone know exactly what's what.

Anyway, back to *that* Wednesday.

The woman who only came down that day hadn't arrived yet, but the whole place seemed to be waiting for her. Everything was quieter than usual on a Wednesday. Sure, some of the usual suspects still barked, but mostly we were all waiting for... *whatever*...

I was standing right by the door to my cage, wondering who would be going today, when the front door opened. It wasn't the woman but Sam who came walking through. I was so happy to see him, I called out to him. And sure enough he smiled and strolled over to me. But as he was about to reach in to rub my head, he saw a note attached to my kennel door and went very still. And his smell went from happy to completely and utterly *wrong*. Can't describe it any better. He started to stink of panic and bad feelings I can't even name. I was trying to catch his attention to make him feel better by whining a little. But he just kept muttering 'Oh no, no, no…' over and over again.

I finally managed to get hold of his hand through the gate and started to lick it. I figured that surely after a good lick or two things wouldn't look quite so bad anymore. But Sam didn't perk up at all. If anything my licking his hand seemed to make matters worse, because he began to cry. And I had never seen him cry before! I licked his hand even harder, and then I stood up on my hind legs to see if I could make him crouch down like he always did and massage my head and the soft bit behind my ears. He usually liked that as much as I did.

But this time he didn't. And not even when I made that mewling sound my mum had always found so irresistible, did he relent. He looked at me and I could tell that he was getting more and more frantic. He looked up the corridor and down the corridor, all the while muttering and chewing his lip and crying. He told me we were running out time and asked no one in particular 'What do I do?' a few times.

Well, here's the problem, humans always do this. They ask us weird questions, but when we answer they don't understand a word of what we're saying. So it's pointless to answer. And pointless to ask us in the first place.

Also, at this particular moment I really didn't understand what all the fuss was about. Sure, it was a Wednesday, sure the atmosphere stank on that day, but after the woman from upstairs had been and done her thing, everything would go back to normal as usual. And I could finally play 'pull' with Sam in the yard again.

Only, Sam didn't think so. I could tell.

There was a clicking sound from upstairs as if someone was walking down the steps to our level at last. And that's when Sam made up his mind and changed the rules of the game as far as Wednesdays were concerned. He moved so fast I almost missed what he was doing.

Before I knew it he had opened the door to my kennel. But instead of clipping my lead on and leading me out into the yard as I half expected he would, he threw one of my blankets over my head, wrapped me all up in it like a parcel, picked me up and started to run. Away from the door that led to the stairs and out through a door I had never been through before. I didn't see where he carried me next because he was running so fast, things went topsy-turvy for a while. Also, by now the blanket was covering my eyes and most of my nose, too.

All the while he kept on running, Sam held me so tight I could hardly breathe. And Sam breathed way too much. But he wouldn't stop running. Not for a long while.

I could feel we were outside because it was getting warmer by the minute. Then again, maybe that was just Sam, sweating right through the blanket in his haste to get away.

After what seemed like ages, he finally slowed down to a walk. And another long while later, he stopped walking altogether and sat down on the floor with me in his arms, still breathing way too fast. And then he put me down on the ground next to him and unwrapped me. At last!

I gulped in a few deep breaths myself and started to pant because it sure had been hot inside the blanket. And then I turned to look at Sam for an explanation, because I just couldn't figure out what had caused him to act this way.

At the same time I noticed that we were somewhere I had never been to before. In a woodland or park of sorts that was much wilder than the park I had visited with Jessica and Joshua. We were sitting in a grassy hollow, and all around us there were trees and bushes, and strange spiky plants with flowers that poked me painfully in the nose when I sniffed them. But there were no other people apart from the two of us. Not sure why. Maybe because it was quite windy and had just started to rain.

Sam was still breathing heavily. He didn't seem to notice the wind and the rain. Or maybe he just didn't care. He just kept looking at me, and at last he smiled, a sad, little, wistful smile that smelled all wrong. And then he hugged and stroked me and even kissed my head. Oh, and he let me lick his face. Which I did. Thoroughly!

Then Sam took a deep breath and did exactly what my mum had always done; he explained to me what was what. At length, and not in baby language. I got most of what he said, but it made me awfully sad, because I understood that he was saying goodbye.

Sam told me that he was sorry he couldn't take care of me, but that surely *this* was better than the alternative. And that he wished things could be different, but that at least this way I had a chance. Oh, and to make sure I took that chance, and whatever I did, NOT TO COME LOOKING FOR HIM!! And especially and most importantly NEVER, EVER to try to go back to the shelter!

He also said 'I'm so sorry, buddy, I didn't know this was going to happen, otherwise I would have brought some food for you.'

Then he wished me good luck, kissed me one last time on top of my head, got up and suddenly, and completely unexpectedly, yelled at me to 'RUUUNNNNN!!!'

And what can I say? I did. Was so startled at what had happened and that Sam had yelled at me right there at the end, that my feet took over and ran away as fast as they could, right into the undergrowth.

I ran and ran and ran. At first because I was scared and upset. Then because I could and for the sheer freedom of running freely at last. And after that, for a long while, simply because I couldn't stop running anymore.

I ran past trees and bushes, over grassy knolls and through mountains of ferns, past little puddles and big puddles. And sometimes right through them.

I ran on muddy tracks and off them, too. Ok, it was more a case of hopping over fallen branches and shrubs like a rabbit when I did that – *now, what was it about rabbits I almost remembered right there…?*

When I finally stopped running, I didn't know where on earth I was. I looked around and realised that the park I was in must be endless. No manicured lawns and children's playgrounds around here. And still no people. But, like I said, maybe that was only because they didn't want to get caught up in the wind and the rain that had been picking up quite a lot since I had started to run.

No sooner had that thought entered my mind, than I realised that I was already wet through and through. It was a completely new sensation. At all the places I had stayed at, the only time I had ever been this wet had been under the shower. Or in the bath. And then never for long, because humans always seem to want to blow-dry you right after they wet you down. Weird! But also kind of handy.

Unfortunately this time there was no one around to dry my fur, so I started to shake myself to get rid of all the water running down my sides.

At first the shaking-and-shaking-and-shaking myself was great fun because there was no one around to screech and tell me off for spraying the water absolutely everywhere. But after a while I realised that no amount of shaking completely dried me off, and with the wind driving the rain harder and harder at me as it did, I only got wet again as soon as I stopped shaking myself.

So I looked around for somewhere to shelter and after a while came across an old tree trunk that was completely overgrown with all sorts of green stuff that was hanging down its side, sort of like a curtain. And when the wind ruffled the green curtain, I suddenly spotted a hollowed-out hidey-hole just behind it. Cautiously and very slowly I stuck first my nose and then my whole head through the green tendrils and the mossy bits, hoping very much they wouldn't hide yet another nasty surprise.

I could immediately tell that someone had been in there before me, but it didn't smell like a dog or a cat. No, the smell was way more pungent than that. It was like nothing I had ever come across before. Luckily for me though, whoever or whatever it had been wasn't around any longer. So I took a chance and ever so slowly crept all the way down into the hole and then tried to make myself as comfortable as possible on the old leaves and the mossy bits that were spread all over the ground.

Unfortunately, the space was far too small for me to stand up properly and shake myself dry. But at least the rain couldn't get to me in my new den. I was shivering quite a lot though and for quite some time under my wet fur, I can tell you! And when I managed to fall asleep at long last, not even the music inside my head could keep me warm.

When I woke up again it was dark. Inside, and outside too, from what I could glimpse through the gaps of the plants covering the entrance to my new den. It was really scary because I couldn't see much at all, and there were *sooooooooo* many strange noises in the night. I didn't know what they were, so I made myself as small as possible and listened warily.

And boy, was I hungry! But because I could hear that the wind was still strong, and the rain even stronger, I didn't dare to go outside to try to find some food. In the end I only left my shelter for a as long as it took to mark the tree in front of it – had to make sure whoever had owned the space before me, knew that it had now been taken – and to quickly drink some water from one of the many puddles. Of course, the minute I did this, I got thoroughly wet again because the wind was lashing the rain all over me.

Back safely inside once more, I lay shivering on my mossy bed and listened to the creaking, squeaking, groaning, cracking, flapping and sloshing all around me that was steadily getting louder and louder. And all the while the wind was howling like crazy, and the rain was pelting the plants outside my den.

When it just wouldn't let up, I tried my very best to ignore the whole pandemonium and was *just* about to nod off despite it all, when all of a sudden there was a dazzlingly bright flash of light, followed by an almighty thunderclap that shocked me wide awake.

I had only ever experienced a thunderstorm once before. It *really* had scared the hell out of me at the time – and that was from the safety of being underneath the sofa in the living room at Jessica and Joshua's.

But this was VERY different. For starters I wasn't safely inside a house. And it all sounded awfully close. And getting closer still.

I was very, very scared. And completely and utterly alone. With no one to hold and stroke me and tell me everything would be alright – not that that had worked particularly well for me in the past – but you know what I mean.

I'm not exactly sure how, but at some stage during all the howling and the lightning and the thunderclaps, my body must have decided to ignore the horrible ruckus and to sleep despite of it.

Because when I next opened my eyes, it was daylight once more and the thunder and lightning had mercifully stopped.

It still rained like mad though, so I only nipped out quickly to do my business, before hurrying back inside as fast as I could. Still didn't dare to leave my shelter for any longer period of time to try and find some food, because I didn't want to get all wet again. But my stomach was growling. LOUDLY. All the way through my endless musings over what had happened with Sam. When it growled so fiercely that I couldn't hear myself think anymore, I decided to go outside in search of some food after all. Just to shut it up.

Of course I immediately got soaking wet, but that just couldn't be helped, and so I tried my best to ignore it.

As soon as I had departed my den, I made sure to mark every other tree, all the way through the woods, so I would be able to find it again when I was done exploring. Unfortunately… in my haste to find something to eat, it simply didn't occur to me that the rain would wash off my scent as quickly as I had laid it on. I guess you could say it was a case of not being able to think straight now that my stomach had taken over. And my stomach didn't care about ANYTHING but to eagerly follow my nose to where it suspected some food could be found.

Turns out there must have been people about in the woodland at some stage after all because I eventually came across a well-trodden path along a swollen river. With lots of litter on the ground all alongside it. And for once I got lucky because, amongst all the rubbish, I found a whole burger someone had carelessly thrown away. It took me ages though to wrestle it out of the bag it was in and then to get at it through the many layers of wrapping. In the end I gave up and simply devoured it all. Wrappings, burger, bits of bag, the lot. Gave me quite a lot of stomach cramps later on, but for now it was just such a relief to finally have something in my belly again.

There were other scraps of food strewn about on the path, but most of them smelled off, so I didn't bother with them. But I did find some soggy fries a little further along. They tasted muddy and had bits of grass on them, but I just didn't care.

Well, not much anyway.

During all this, the rain didn't let up once and the wind was well on its way to becoming a proper storm, which is why I figured it was high time to make my way back to my makeshift den.

The only problem was that the rain had of course by now washed away all my markings, and I seriously started to panic when I couldn't find them any longer. And then, all of a sudden, I heard a loud whining sound that startled me and made me jump... until I realised that it was coming out of my own throat. But no amount of whining could help me find my shelter again. I desperately searched for it, this way and that way, but couldn't find my way back there.

The wind was positively roaring by now and I had trouble keeping my paws firmly on the ground. I was wet through and through and didn't know what to do. In my desperation I tried to dig my way into some shrubs but only managed to badly scratch my nose and face on the spiky thorns I hadn't realised were covering the branches.

I also tried to squeeze inside a hole at the base of an old tree. Alas, to no avail. The hole was way too small and I almost got my head stuck inside it.

Then, as I was finally running out of ideas, a

miracle happened and, against all the odds, I found my den again. Stumbled right over it, to be precise, and only recognised it by my own smell when I did.

I was so utterly relieved, I began to shake all over. Couldn't stop shaking no matter how hard I tried. Might have even wet myself. Ok, so yes, I did.

I also couldn't stop whining, even when I was safely back inside once more. But at the same time I was so very happy I had found my shelter again, I almost forgot how hungry I still was. Just scraped the leaves and the mossy bits on the ground into a comfy nest as best I could, lay down on top of them and fell asleep almost at once.

But, like so often in life, my luck didn't hold.

Halfway through the night, I woke up coughing and spluttering. Couldn't get my bearings at all or remember where I was because there was now water everywhere inside my den. And more came flooding in, in small, lapping waves. Where I had been lying, it now almost came up to my chin.

Utterly panicked, I scrambled up and out of the opening as fast as I could. Had to duck under the water that came pouring in steadily to do so.

Outside wasn't any better. There were now

deep water puddles everywhere. Even the path a bit further along was completely flooded. I had to paddle across it to get to the higher ground. Once there, I didn't dare to rest. Just in case I would fall asleep and drown. Not that there was much of a chance of me falling asleep in the midst of the deluge.

I was so wet and cold I couldn't feel my paws any longer. So I did the only thing left to me – I started to walk.

Can't tell you how long I walked – seemed like forever. Walked right through the wind and the rain, too tired at long last to care about all the scary noises around me. Also can't tell you when the rain finally stopped, and the sun came up. Just kept walking. I only stopped when the path I was on ended abruptly and I could go no further. Because right there in front of me was the sea. I only know that's what it was because no sooner had I clapped eyes on it than my brain went into overdrive... I *knew* this somehow... *salt and fishy smells in the air... sooooo many pebbles... and someone throwing them just for me... someone who loved me an awful, awful lot... and feeling* Home...

I sat down on the rocky ground and stared.

For ages.

But nothing else revealed itself to me. I looked at the sea stretching out in front of me. And remembered that it was the sea. But I also *knew* that it was the wrong sea and the wrong place. This place was vaguely similar, but not at all the same.

I didn't know what to do.

Chapter 6

LOST

I sat for quite some time among the shrubs on the gravelly sand and watched the sea, hoping I would remember more. When nothing of the sort happened, I got up and looked around.

There was a lot of garbage people had thrown away, all around me. Mostly useless, filthy, rotten stuff. Lots of wrappers, bottles and empty cans. But luckily for me, also bits of old bread. I gobbled them up in a hurry even though they were soggy and mouldy. In fact, I ate *all* I could find, even if it smelled off. Was just way too hungry to stop myself.

I never knew you could be so hungry you simply wouldn't care what you ate any longer. Memories of the yummy strips of steak The Girlfriend had given me sure seemed a lifetime away.

When I had eaten all the scraps around and drunk some water from one of the many puddles, I turned my back on the sea and walked right back into the undergrowth beneath the trees once more.

I walked for ages before I suddenly came across a funny looking building with lots of colours and weird shapes painted all across the walls. I sneaked closer, thinking that maybe someone lived there who had some food they would share with me. But it was only an empty shell of a building that didn't even have doors or windows. Only open squares in the walls where the windows should have been, and a staircase leading down into a dilapidated room of sorts. It would have made a great refuge had the whole place not been full of water. And there were no people anywhere in sight. Can't say that I liked the place much. It smelled strange. Made me not want to go inside. Luckily it had stopped raining, so I didn't need to.

I found a knoll of grass nearby that was dry enough and lay down on it. Trampled it flat in the middle first, by going round and round and round in circles – as you do – then lay down and fell asleep.

I woke up because some birds were making an awful lot of noise. And that's when I suddenly heard voices. People, talking, coming closer. I was in two minds as to what to do. Didn't want to risk falling into the hands of someone like the two men who had stolen and then sold me, but I also was rather desperate for some proper food. And company, if I'm honest.

Mind made up at last, I decided to walk in their direction. Make that limp – my paws were still aching an awful lot from all the walking the day and night before.

Now, we will never know if the people would have helped me or not, because something about the way they smelled made me change my mind at the very last moment. *Just* before they came into sight, I dropped down to the ground, flat on my belly, and stayed very, very still.

Hidden by the brush and the long grass, I watched a group of young men and women walk right past without spotting me. I liked their smell even less as they got closer, so I stayed where I was until they passed me by. And then I waited until I couldn't see or hear them any longer.

Problem was, my tummy happened to disagree with my decision. It growled and growled and wouldn't stop growling, until I finally got up to try and find some food to make it stop.

Can't tell you how long I walked that day either. There were plenty of puddles around so I didn't get thirsty, but whatever scraps of food I found amongst all the litter near the paths, never filled my belly completely. Not even close!

Also, as soon as the sun came out from behind the clouds, it was getting really hot and sticky, and I soon was covered from top to toe in tiny flies that kept bothering my eyes and my nose. And no amount of snapping ever got rid of them. Trying to scratch them off with my paws didn't help either. Only managed to scratch my eyes and nose some more.

By the time the sun went down, I was feeling very weak and woozy. My eyes and nose hurt, and my paws were swollen and had started to bleed in places. So I found myself a dry place on the higher ground under some trees to try to lick them better. Really soothing, licking your paws – you ought to try it sometime!

Got a bit carried away with it though, which made my paws look even more pink and swollen. Also, by now my tongue had gone numb in my relentless effort to clean myself. And once again, there was just *something* about the whole paw-licking-thing that *almost* made me remember. I could have sworn I had licked my paws in the past like that before…

I didn't dwell on it though as I was WAY too tired for that. Since it wasn't raining any longer, I was very much tempted to just stay where I was for the night. But once again, as soon as it was dark, I began to hear all sorts of scary noises and to smell weird and unknown smells. Wild and musty, and really pungent, too. Rather like the smell that had lingered inside my den the night before. And since I didn't want to meet whoever or whatever it was that smelled that way, I dragged myself through the undergrowth once more to try and find another den or hidey-hole.

In the end I came across some bushes covered in vines and flowers that someone else had dug an entrance into. I sniffed around for a while to make sure no one was using it, but since I couldn't smell anyone else but me, I pushed my way in cautiously, carefully trying to avoid all the spiky thorns covering the vines.

Right at the bottom of the bushes was a nest of sorts. I had to cower low and make myself very small to fit into it, but I figured it was better than nothing and made do. Can't say I slept very well because it was rather tight in there, but at least it felt safe.

Right at the bottom of the bushes was a nest of sorts. I had to cower low and make myself very small to fit into it, but I figured it was better than nothing and made do. Can't say I slept very well because it was rather tight in there, but at least it felt safe.

A few hours later, I woke up from my uneasy slumber with a start because I heard a strange noise that sounded *way* too close for comfort. In my panic however I completely forgot where I was and stupidly jumped up to get ready to run if needs be. Unfortunately, as a result of this I became totally entangled in the thorny vines. Also got mightily scratched all over at the same time. And no amount of licking afterwards made it any better. And that's just the bits I could get to.

The next morning I was so very tired I could barely get up. My back and face and paws stung mightily from all the scratches I was sporting, and I was so famished that even my stomach had given up its constant growling.

I only limped along because I didn't know what else to do.

The area I was now in was wilder, with no paths, which meant no litter from people. Which also meant no food scraps for me.

I stumbled around for ages and had almost given up, when at last I found a path again. This one was very muddy but at least it wasn't under water and it made it easier for me to walk along. For a while. Then my paws and underbelly got REALLY muddy. All my open sores were caked with the stuff. Which made them hurt a great deal more.

I tried to lick myself all over to make it better, but that only made my tongue all muddy, too. And now my stomach was protesting again.

In the end I simply gave up and lay down. Because there was nothing else to do. The birds were singing – or rather screeching – and I just listened to them for a while until at last I dozed off. Didn't care about anything any longer. Didn't even have the energy to feel scared anymore. Just dozed. And dozed.

I'm not sure what woke me up, but when I looked around I could see something moving in the distance, further down the muddy path. At first, I thought I was imagining things, but then things became clearer and I could see two couples walking hand in hand, slowly making their way towards where I was lying on the ground.

I heard myself whimper before I could stop myself. Didn't get up, just kept whimpering. As I told you, I was pretty much past caring whether they were friend or foe by then. I was just desperate for this nightmare to end. Any which way.

They must have heard me whimper though because the next thing I knew they had started to hurry towards me. I heard one of the men tell the others to be careful in case I was dangerous. I mean, *really*?!! There I was, half dead on the ground, covered from top to toe in sores and mud – and flies! – and they were worried about Rule Number One! I couldn't have imposed that even if I wanted to. And, let me tell you, I was MILES past it!

So then, one of the women sticks out her hand and let's me sniff it. And when I didn't bite it off she proceeded to stroke my head. Which was ever so soothing and made me close my eyes to savour the feeling. Hadn't been stroked like that in a while.

Through it all I could tell the people were getting a bit frantic in their worry for me. I was so relieved they were good, kind people I stayed very still even when they tried to move me.

I could smell they didn't have any food on them, but I didn't care about that any longer. It was just *sooooooo* nice to have someone take care of me again.

Now, I wish I could tell you, that that was the end of all my troubles and everything was coming up roses after that. But sadly I can't. That nasty part of life my mum always hated so much, wasn't quite done with me yet.

Because, as all four of them took turns to talk to me and stroke me, I heard one of the men say, 'We have to call the animal shelter. They will be able to help him…'

Can't remember what else he said, but as soon as I heard him say the word 'shelter', I remembered that Sam had told me to 'NEVER, EVER go back to the shelter!' that time he said goodbye to me for the last time. And even though I still didn't understand completely what had happened back then, I just *knew* he was right.

In fact I panicked so badly when I heard that the people meant to take me back to the horrible shelter, I found a last bit of energy deep down inside myself. Didn't know I had anything left in me, until I scrambled up and frantically twisted my head away from whoever was holding me. Then I somehow got on my feet and started to run away from the people as fast as my shaking legs would carry me.

I must have really taken them completely by surprise because for the first few seconds they didn't do anything to try and stop me. And when they were finally galvanised into action, I was already too far down the track for them to catch up with me. Because they were much heavier than I, and the mud made it harder for them to run.

Fear gave me such a tremendous burst of energy that even though they tried their hardest, they just couldn't stop or catch me. I blindly ran on, didn't look back, and blanked out all the shouting and commotion behind me.

I ran and ran, down the path, off the path, up the slope, right through a thicket of trees, and almost flew out the other end in my frantic effort to get away.

Only... I hadn't realised that I had finally reached the end of the woodlands, and as I desperately propelled myself out of the thicket, I hit the road that had been hidden from sight behind the trees.

There was a roar in my head and an almighty roar in the air.

I didn't really see the car that hit me, I only felt it. It slammed hard into my side and then my back twisted, my paws went right out from under me and I was flung though the air. Like a stuffed toy when you shake it too hard and then suddenly let it go.

I hit the road on the far side with a painful thud.

The last thing I remember is rolling over and over until I finally landed in the ditch.

Then everything went black.

Well, not *completely*. Not really. Because, you see, at the same time it did, this bright, bright light came on. In an almighty flash. And with it, TONS of pictures and... *FEELINGS*... came flooding in. So many of them, I felt like drowning. And they filled my head and my heart with *sooooooooooooooo* many memories.

And I remembered EVERYTHING.

Every last little thing I had forgotten for so long.

I remembered all about my last life, the one I had led before I had been born again in the wrong country. And all about my time on the Other Side, where I had made a wish and promised myself that I would REMEMBER and find my parents again.

I remembered good things and bad things, important things and silly things, big things and the tiniest things. All in an instant.

But most of all I remembered my mum and dad, and how I had first met them at the RSPCA rescue centre, that beautiful spring day in April so many years ago. I remembered how I had fallen in love with them right there and then, and they with me. And how I had realised in that very instant that they were my forever family. Forever.

I remembered my mum singing and laughing and telling me over and over that she loved me during the many years that followed. I remembered my dad telling me the same, just not out loud, but with every little stroke of his hand and every look into my eyes, and everything he did for me. I remembered listening to the music he composed, that filled the whole house *and* my heart and made my mum cry happy tears. And I realised at last that it had been my dad's music I had been hearing in my dreams during all the time I couldn't remember anything else.

I also remembered my *Home*, and every last little detail about it. The many stairs going up and down, and that I could watch the sea and the people in the street below from my favourite spot on my sofa – and tell them off for waving at me of course.

I remembered my two grandmas and all my favourite aunts and uncles, and that they had loved me too, no matter what. Even when I wasn't exactly on my best behaviour – which, admittedly... um... was most of the time...

And of course I remembered why I had come up with Rule Number One, right after the vet had stuck a needle into my unsuspecting bottom.

I remembered my walks in the Country Park in Hastings, up on the East Hill, right behind our house, and how my mum used to bend down all the way to the ground, looking back at me through her legs, calling out to me. And how I would run over to her at the speed of lightning and dart right through her open legs because I knew she wanted me to. Ok, so *sometimes* I would. And sometimes I wouldn't. Depending on the mood I was in. I'm not a wind-up toy, you know! Or a circus dog.

I remembered the beach by our house, and all the pebbles and sticks my dad had ever thrown for me.

I remembered all the good times my parents and I had had together. And all the *mimos* – you know, cuddles – and kisses we had shared.

But of course I also remembered the bad times, and how I had gotten ill and finally lost my leg. How my parents had desperately tried to save me, but just couldn't because the cancer had been so much stronger than they and all the vets in the world put together. And how our good times together finally had come to an end.

I also remembered watching my mum and dad from the Other Side after I had died. Watching them cry and miss me terribly. And that I couldn't let them know I was still around and lick their faces to make things better.

I remembered meeting all my other furry siblings on the Other Side – the ones I'd never met because they all died before I arrived on the scene. And I remembered finding out all about their own stories, too.

And finally, I remembered my dad telling me to

make a wish when he and my mum were celebrating my 12th birthday – the one I never had. And how I had closed my eyes and wished with all my heart and let the link that goes from my heart to theirs pull me right back to them, only to end up in a completely different country and so very far away from *Home*.

Memories are a funny thing. They wrap you up until you're all warm inside and fill your soul with happiness. But they also hurt. And not just a bit. Because by remembering the good times, you also know what you don't have any longer.

And in that moment when I remembered everything at last, I missed my mum and dad so very, very much, my heart began to ache even more than my back.

And then everything went completely black.

Chapter 7

THE OLD LADY

When I opened my eyes again I was in a world of pain. My back was all twisted and I couldn't get up.

Then I noticed that I wasn't alone. An old lady was sitting right next to me on the grass. And she was stroking me all over. With very shaky hands.

I could tell that she was very, very upset because she was crying a lot. I heard her sob 'No, no, no, no, no!' over and over again. And, 'Stay with me, darlin'! *Please!*' As soon as she said that I almost got up on my feet.

Well, I would have, if I could have.

Because the way she spoke sounded awfully similar to the way some people spoke back *Home*. Not quite the same, but similar. It was something in the way she talked. Not *what* she said, but *how* she said it. She sounded nothing like the people I had met in this country.

But my body just wouldn't move, so I just listened to the familiar lilt whilst she kept stroking me, and let her voice lull me to sleep.

I don't remember the in-between, but when I came to, I looked around and – what do you know – I was back at the vet's!!!

Didn't know this one, and was too weak to crawl away from him, so I let him do whatever he wanted to do. Which, OF COURSE, involved – you've guessed correctly! – sticking needles into my bottom! Unbelievable!!

This time though I didn't mind when everything went fuzzy. I let myself sink right back into my memories and knew no more.

When I came around again, I wasn't over on the Other Side as I had half expected. Instead I was in a cage once more. With a plastic cone around my neck and a lot of my hair missing.

I panicked immediately because I thought for a moment I was back at the shelter. Must have yowled out loud in my dismay, because a young nurse came rushing in to check on me.

I didn't recognise her, so I figured I was still at the vet's. Especially since it smelled similar to the place where they had taken my leg off in my last life. That thought made me panic again and I quickly sat up and looked down to check if any of my legs were missing. And boy, was I relieved to find that this time around nobody had stolen any of my limbs! And all the rest of me was wobbly but seemed to be working alright, too.

But whatever the vet had given me, made me so woozy I had to lie down again. Ok, so I keeled right over, to tell you the truth.

The next few days passed in a haze. I was always drifting in and out of consciousness, all the while pretending to myself that I was right back *Home* with my family.

In between the sleeping and the dreaming, the nurses took me out of my cage to see if I could stand. Which OF COURSE I could. I'm not an idiot! Ok, so admittedly I couldn't do it for more than a second or two, and they insisted on putting a sling around my body to take the weight off my shaking legs and help me walk. That first time I almost couldn't do it, but in time luckily things got better.

Oh, and I found out that the nurses shared all humans' obsession with dog poo. Remember, that I once told you that it must be worth a lot, judging by the way people always rush to pick it up?

Well, you should have seen how happy they were at the vet's when I pooed at last! One nurse called out to another nurse, who ran to fetch the vet. And then they all stood there, laughing and smiling, hugging each other and squeezing each other's arms. The vet even high-fived one of the nurses.

Whilst looking at my poo!

Human's are so weird! I could have told them there was always more where that came from.

I stayed at the vet's for an awfully long time and slowly I was beginning to wonder what would happen next. Ok, make that worry myself sick – because I *REALLY* didn't want to go back to the nasty shelter. I was still in a lot of pain and had to move way more slowly than before. Also, my hind legs were still giving out from time to time, whenever I was taken by the nurses for my short, daily walks outside in the yard. Not sure why it kept happening, but it was highly annoying.

But on the bright side, I had finally plenty of food again. And most importantly, I had my memories back.

Then, one morning, right after breakfast, one of the nurses got me out of my cage, and I could tell from the way she smelled that things were coming to an end as far as my stay at the vet's was concerned. She picked me up and carried me to another room. And yes, before you ask, I let her. Somewhere along the way, and to my own surprise, I had decided I wasn't going to enforce Rule Number One any longer. Figured *mimos* were far more important – and urgently required – than silly rules that only got me into trouble.

We got to the room with the table in the middle where I always met the vet. And sure enough, there he was, standing right beside it, waiting for me.

But someone else was also standing there – the old lady who had found me beside the road after I had been hit by the car. I sure was happy to see her. She was nothing like my mum, but something about the way she looked at me reminded me of her. As soon as the nurse put me down on the table in front of the vet, the old lady walked right up to me and began to stroke my face and my back. And I wagged my tail like mad and let her cuddle me. Was so happy to see her that I licked her face when she kissed my head.

And before I could start to wonder why she was here, and to worry if this was only another goodbye, she took my head into her hands, looked deep into my eyes and asked me if I wanted to come home and live with her.

Did I ever??!!!

I guess if I had been human I would have cried for joy. As I wasn't, I whimpered. And then I licked the old lady's hands and face as thoroughly as I could. And I guess she got my answer.

After that the vet carried me to her car. I heard him give the old lady all sorts of instructions on how to help me recover along the way. But I didn't listen to any of it. I was just SO happy that I had finally someone who was going to take care of me again. Sure, the old lady wasn't my mum and dad.

But she was the closest bit to *Home* I had had in a long, long time.

We drove for quite some time, me in the back of the car, and the old lady in the front, and the purring of the car made me all sleepy again. So I snoozed for a while, relieved that I was safe at last.

I dreamt of my mum and dad. We were all back together again, lounging around on my sofa. My mum was nibbling my ear and telling me she loved me for the umpteenth time. And my dad was laughing as I tried to bury my head under his thigh to get away from the never-ending nibbling. Well, not really. Deep down I loved it, but you can get too much of a good thing. And my mum never knows when to stop when it comes to *mimos*.

I wanted to stay with them forever, but unfortunately I woke up. Just as the car came to a halt.

The old lady opened the door to the back of the car and looked at me. I looked right back at her. And then she smiled. The kind of smile that told that me she was *really* happy to see me. She smelled really happy, too. It made me want to lick her face again. She must have understood, because she sat down next to me and let me do just that. She had to bend down to my level because my back didn't let me stretch up that far. Then she told me that we had arrived at my new home, and to 'Wait a moment!' while she got the ramp. Wasn't sure what she meant, but my back was aching fiercely again, so I stayed put and waited for her to come back.

Whatever the vet had given me to make the pain go away was definitely beginning to wear off. Made me way less woozy and I finally could think straight again, but the trade-off wasn't exactly great.

When the old lady came back she was carrying a plank of wood which she leaned against the back of the car, so it formed a walkway down to the ground. Then she smiled again and told me 'There y' go, darlin', here's your very own ramp. See if y' can manage to walk down. Unfortunately I'm too old and you're too heavy for me to lift y' down.'

I hadn't realised how wobbly my legs were until I was midway down the makeshift ramp. Had to concentrate mightily not to fall off it. And definitely couldn't have jumped down from the car if the old lady hadn't put the plank there for me.

We were both relieved and very happy when I

made it all the way down without a tumble. I got a 'Well, done, darlin'!' and a tasty treat for my efforts. And then I followed the old lady up the path to a small white house among the trees. She opened the front door for me and in we went together.

My mum always used to say things like 'This jumper is *so* like you!' or 'These shoes are *so* like you!' to people, and I never really fully understood what she meant. But when I saw the old lady's house I finally got it. Because the house was *so* like the old lady. Friendly and warm and welcoming, and… well *just* like her. And it was nothing like any of the places I had stayed at before in this life.

For starters it was full of things. And I mean FULL. There weren't many toys, but then I didn't feel like playing anyway. There were knick-knacks and ornaments everywhere. And a sofa in the living room with loads of all kinds of woollen blankets and cushions on it. Now, normally I would have jumped up in a flash, but somehow deep down I knew I couldn't do it.

My back felt strange and my legs were weak and achy. Luckily the old lady had thought of everything. There was a doggie bed, just for me, next to the sofa. It wasn't like the one I'd had back home, but it looked very comfy nonetheless.

But before I could try it out, the old lady called out for me to follow her. I was in more pain now, and every step hurt, but I was also very curious.

Turns out the old lady must have heard my tummy rumble because, as we entered the kitchen where she was taking me, there were two bowls on the floor, with paws painted on them, just like the ones I used to have back home. And one of the bowls was full of the nicest smelling food.

I didn't hang about much, I can tell you! Hobbled right over and gulped down the lot, as fast as I could.

Yep, turns out that day was almost perfect, as days without my mum and dad go.

After the meal the old lady showed me around the house. We went from room to room and out into the back garden. And she explained what everything was.

When we came back in I tried out my new doggie bed. To make the old lady happy. But even though I really appreciated the trouble she had gone to getting it for me, I just couldn't help but gaze up longingly at the sofa where she was sitting. And once again the old lady understood immediately. Got up straight away, went outside and came back with the plank from the car, which she then leaned against the seat of the sofa. Then she sat down once more and patted the space right next to her to entice me to walk up the plank.

I didn't really need any enticing – stumbled up the ramp as quickly as my wobbly feet allowed, and made myself comfortable right next to her.

The old lady then covered me with one of her many blankets – just like my parents would have done. And I happily went to sleep by her side.

We spent most of that afternoon on the sofa, and I snoozed for most of the time because I just felt so safe and happy in her company. And the old lady must have felt the same because after a while I could hear her gently snoring away.

We didn't go for walkies that day. I did my business in the back garden under the trees. It was a lovely garden, but I was far too tired to explore it. And also, I figured, there would be plenty of time for that.

Just before we went to bed that evening, after yet more yummy food and treats, the old lady gave me some pills to make the pain go away. I knew that's what they were because she did the same thing my parents used to do – she wrapped them in some ham to trick me into taking them. But she needn't have bothered. I could have easily unwrapped and spat them out if I wanted to. I was a master at that, if you remember. But because I now remembered everything, I of course also knew *why* my mum and dad had given me pills in the past.

And so I took them. And pretended not to have noticed what was hidden inside the ham. To make the old lady feel good.

She smiled at me, and then she let me out into the garden for the final time that day. When we came back inside, she showed me the way to our bedroom. It was a lovely room, as full of things as the living room, with a bed on one side and an armchair on the other, with tons of pillows on it. And – can you believe it – she had even bought a second doggie bed for me and put it right next to her bed. So I would have a bed for the day in the living room, and another one for the night to sleep in, as she explained to me. It was the nicest thing anyone had done for me in a very long time. And I sure was grateful.

But alas… as nice as the doggie bed was… it was never to be used by me.

Because, you see, the old lady simply couldn't resist my mournful look as I stood silently by the side of her bed, as soon as she had gotten into it.

So, back to the living room she traipsed to get the plank for me once more. And no sooner had she leaned it against her bed, than I staggered up it as fast as I could and got into bed right next to her. Snuggled up as close to her as I possibly could and never slept anywhere else during the nights after that.

Which made us both very happy.

During the days and months that followed, the old lady and I got to know each other very well. And although I missed my parents an awful lot, deep down I now knew that I would never be able to find my way back home to them all by myself. Because I had ended up in the wrong country, and it was MILES away from my old Home. With a whole big ocean in between.

But I also remembered that my parents had visited North America before, on one of their many trips without me, and so I clung to the hope that they would do so again, and miraculously come find me.

But… it didn't happen.

And over the years that followed I slowly began to wonder if I would ever see them again.

The old lady and I settled into a whole new routine starting the morning after my arrival at her house. She would get up early, and I would stay buried deep inside the duvet and the blankets and not get up until I heard her call 'Come on, darlin', breakfast is ready!'

After breakfast and a quick pee in the garden – me, not her – we would go for a walk. Never too long, never too far – and slowly, ever so slowly, because I couldn't run like I could before. I did get stronger over time but it was never again quite the same as before.

After our morning walkies, we both had a nap. Then the old lady had lunch, and so did I. After that we sat in the garden. She had her tea, and I had a bone to chew on.

The evenings were spent reading (her) and snoozing (me) on the sofa. And like I told you, afterwards we then shared the bed and cuddled up during the night.

On some days she took me to see places in the car. And once or twice to the vet's. But I wasn't so scared of him anymore. Because I knew the old lady would never let any harm come to me. And that she would never leave me behind.

During all that time, we never really met up with any other people. Not to hang out with anyhow. I guess the old lady didn't have many friends. But I reckon, my mum and dad would have been friends with her had they known her.

Luckily for me, the old lady was almost as fond of *mimos* as my parents had been. She also never stopped talking to me. Just like my mum. Well, maybe even more than my mum. Because she had been lonely during the many years she had been all by herself. But now she had me to keep her company. And so she talked and talked, all day long, now that she finally had someone to talk to once more.

She told me all about herself and how she 'hailed from a different shore'. She told me how green the island had been where she grew up, and that she missed the rain and the mist that was so common over there. Couldn't really relate to that one, but I did remember the rain and mist well from my own old *Home*.

The old lady also told me all about a great big war and the hardships she and her family had had to endure afterwards. And of her joy when she found happiness at last and fell in love with a young man called Bertie. She kept telling me 'He was such a handsome young fellow', and wouldn't stop smiling as she did so. She even showed me photographs of him.

Lots of them.

I heard an awful lot about Bertie during the months and years that followed. On a daily basis. How he looked, how he walked, what he said, and that he was 'a charmer, that one, and such a good kisser'. I heard all about their life together and how happy they had been.

And then I heard all about the 'great adventure' when they both decided to move half a world away. The old lady told me how very different life was over here. I could have told her the same.

She also told me how she and Bertie would have loved to have children but that it wasn't to be. 'Not for want of trying, y' understand, my darlin'?' she giggled. And then she giggled some more until she laughed and laughed, and only when I saw tears streaming down her face did I realise that she wasn't laughing any longer. I had to lick her hand and face a lot to make her feel better.

The old lady also told me how one day Bertie had gotten sick, and wouldn't get better again. No matter how hard he tried. No matter how hard *she* tried. And that no matter how much she had begged him to stay, he just couldn't. He died and left her behind. All alone and by herself.

At this stage she would always add, 'I was very lonely after he died. But then I found you, my darlin'. And what a fright y' gave me at first!' Then the old lady would pause and stroke my head and face and look me in the eyes and whisper, 'And I'm so very glad you stayed!'

Chapter 8

TWISTS AND TURNS

We sure had a lovely time together, the old lady and I, and it was so very, very nice to have someone again at last who cared for me and loved me, no matter what.

That's one thing I learned during this life; you can never have enough love. Even when you miss it like crazy when it's gone. And you can never have enough *mimos* either.

I never misbehaved in all the time I spent with the old lady. Not at first when I was slowly getting better every day, and not later on either. Because I didn't need to. And also because somehow I was past all that.

Time flew by so quickly it was startling. Don't know exactly how much time passed though. Back *Home* I had been able to tell the seasons by the wind and the rain, followed by *slightly* warmer weather and my parents taking me to the beach for a swim. Well, ok, *they* swam, whilst I stood and barked at them from the edge of the water to 'GET OUT ALREADY AND THROW ME SOME PEBBLES!!'. And sometimes my mum would trick me by distracting me with lots of *mimos* and then quickly scooping me up into her arms and carrying me out into the water before I could object. Sneaky or what?!!

Of course that only worked once every season or so, because I became wise to what she was up to and showed her my teeth as soon as I had paddled back and was safely on land once more. To make sure there wasn't a repeat performance of her trickery.

I also used to be able to tell the passage of time by Christmas coming around again. Because of the tree my mum and dad got down from the attic for that occasion, which they then decorated with tons of baubles and other dangly bits. And because Heloir, the little toy deer my parents always placed under it, made his yearly reappearance, and I was told to 'Leave it!' whenever I got within nipping distance.

And of course I could tell the time of year because the weather was cold, wet and miserable once more.

But over here, where the old lady and I lived, it was mainly very hot, then less hot, then warm, then very hot again. And in between it was windy – much more windy than back *Home*. With storms that twisted the trees and the houses and flooded everything. Wasn't too happy whenever that happened. Not at all. Because it reminded me of the horrible time I had spent in the woods before the old lady had found me.

Of course, the old lady also celebrated Christmas. But she only had a tiny tree in a pot with lots of tinsel on it – and no Heloir for anyone to nip beneath it. Still, I got many yummy treats, all wrapped up in tons of colourful paper to make them a surprise – not that it was a surprise *really* because OF COURSE I could smell a mile off what was in each parcel – even before I began to unwrap it. Still, it made the old lady happy to watch me get at my presents and so I humoured her.

We also had turkey dinner. With lots of gravy on it. Still salivating, just thinking about it.

For the longest time though I didn't know the old lady's name. Because no one came to visit her and so no one ever said her name. And although she talked to me a lot, she never told me what she was called. Well, apart from that one time when she told me that she was 'a daft old duck' – which was very confusing because I knew for a fact that she wasn't. No feathers for starters. And even though ducks also walk on two legs, surely she must have know that she was human!

So for ages I only thought of her as 'the old lady'.

Until, one day, she accidentally dropped her tea cup and it smashed to smithereens on the kitchen floor. I would have known it was her favourite cup, even if she hadn't wailed out loud 'OH *NOOOOOOOOOO*!!! NOT MY FAVOURITE CUP!!!' Because she always used it for her tea. Never once did she use any of the other cups that were hanging from the wooden cup tree. Only this one. It was old and stained, and much loved.

And now it was no more.

It was truly heart breaking to hear her sob over it the way she did. It really must have been a very special cup. I was very shocked because I had never seen the old lady cry like that before. So I just stood there and watched her sob her heart out, sitting next to what was left of the cup, on the kitchen floor. But when she just wouldn't stop her crying, I sidled over to lick her better. Luckily that did the trick and stopped her desperate sobbing.

She stroked my head, and then she whispered, 'Oh darlin', I'm sorry. I didn't mean to scare y'. Never you mind this silly old biddy!'

And just like that I finally knew her name: Old Biddy. I was so happy she had finally told me her name, I licked her face some more.

Sadly though, she never knew my name was Nelson. And I couldn't tell her. She named me Paddy, after her brother Pádraic, on the day she adopted me at the vet's, but she never really called me that. She called me '*Mo ghrá*' and '*A stór*' and 'my sweet'. But mostly she called me 'darlin', and I knew that meant she loved me. So I reckoned it was okay to let her call me that.

And sometimes just before she went to sleep she would whisper softly '*Is ceol mo chroí thú*', which she once told me means 'You are the music of my heart'. But I was never sure if she meant me or Bertie, because she only said it when she was already half asleep. And I also never knew if that meant that she could hear my dad's music in her dreams like I could.

The hot seasons and the warm seasons and the thunderstorms and hurricanes came and went and came and went, in a never-ending loop.

And still I remembered my old life.

And still I hoped to find my parents again.

But don't get me wrong, I was also happy with the old lady. We kept each other company and had great times together. We picnicked in the garden, and in a park near her house. We went for longer and longer walks while I got stronger again. And I taught her how to throw sticks for me. I couldn't wrestle them with her, like with my dad, because she didn't have the strength to lift me up by my teeth. Mind you, my back would probably have broken again if she had.

We had fun every day, and I felt safe and warm and loved. And not once did she shout at me and tell me off for something, or lock me in the laundry room. Not even when I chewed a hole in her favourite blanket – by accident, I swear!! I had been thinking about the two men who stole me at the airport at the time, and just couldn't help but grind my teeth like mad. *Unfortunately...* I happened to have Old Biddy's blanket in my mouth at that moment...

Old Biddy and I sat together, ate together, walked together and slept together. In fact, we spent almost every single second of the day together. We even had an unintended sleep-over in the garden one night, when Old Biddy pulled the front door shut and forgot the key inside by accident. She yelped, and then she laughed. It was a balmy night and she told me it would be too late to call for help on a Sunday night. So we slept in the garden on the swinging sofa instead. Side by side. The swinging made me feel thoroughly seasick after a while, but I didn't want to leave her side and so I stayed.

More time flew by in a pleasant haze.

And then, one sunny summer's morning, life did that thing again my mum hates so much – it threw us a massive curveball. One day everything was fine and hunky-dory. And then it wasn't.

Just like that.

I remember walking up just before Old Biddy did, and rolling onto my back to stretch myself fully awake. My back felt so much better these days, with only the occasional twinge when I overdid it. My legs were stronger again, too, and I didn't even need the ramp any longer to get up onto the bed and the sofa.

As I was busily stretching away, and scratching my back at the same time, all of a sudden I noticed an *off* smell. No better way to describe it. A smell that wasn't right, and didn't belong.

At first I thought it had drifted in from outside, but when I followed my nose, it led me right over to where Old Biddy was sleeping. I sniffed again. Yep, there it was, seeping out of her snoring mouth. And even though it was only very faint, it smelled awfully *wrong*. And awfully like my shoulder had smelled back in my other life, around the time when I got sick. Before the vet took my leg off.

Remembering that completely freaked me out. I licked Old Biddy's face and mouth to make the bad smell go away. But all it did was wake her up. She smiled, and said 'Well, good morning, darlin'. What a lovely way to wake me up!' And then she kissed my face, right next to my nose, just like my mum always used to do. But all I could think of was the awful smell, stronger now that she was talking to me. And there was no way I could lick it off. Or tell her why I was getting so frantic over it. And believe you me, I tried. But she just didn't understand why I was nudging her and wouldn't stop nudging her.

In the end I could only watch her as day by day the horrible smell got stronger and stronger.

And then, one day, Old Biddy started to cough. She told me she had a cold, and how lucky I was to be a dog so I didn't get any colds. But I just *knew* she didn't have a cold, even though part of me still hoped she might be right.

When the coughing got worse, and the remedies she brewed didn't make things any better, Old Biddy made a long phone call in the kitchen one day. When she came back into the living room and sat down on the sofa next to me, she stroked me a lot. And then she said 'Sorry, darlin', I have to go see the doctor to get some proper medicine, to see me right.' And then she explained at length why she couldn't take me with her and told me to 'be a good boy and wait' until she came back home.

It sure was a long wait for me that day. Old Biddy had never left me alone before. Not in the house anyhow. But because I was more worried about the bad smell than being alone, I stuck it out without complaining. Just sat there by the front door, hoping that the doctor would take the smell away.

When Old Biddy came home at last we both had a cuddle and a good cry. Well, she did, and I was whining along. And then she gave me something to eat. But I noticed that she didn't eat anything herself. And the bad smell was still with her.

After that she seemed to be waiting for something. I know this, because she was absent-minded all the time and kept looking at the phone a lot. I couldn't snap her out of it, so I just waited with her.

When the phone call she must have been waiting for finally came, she hurried into the kitchen to pick it up. I heard her talking, but mainly she just listened.

And after she put the phone down at last, she sat at the kitchen table for a long, long time, with her head in her hands. She didn't cry – not then – but just sat there. And that was so much more horrible than if she had screamed and shouted. Because then I knew for a fact that the bad smell would never go away again. And because I remembered what had happened to myself in my other life, I also knew what that meant.

So we both sat and didn't know what to do. She at the kitchen table. And I by her side with my head pressed tightly against her leg.

She didn't talk to me much that evening. But then no words were needed. We cuddled up on the sofa, and Old Biddy silently stroked and stroked me until it was time to go to bed. Don't know how we managed to sleep that night, but we both did. And my dad's music, deep inside my heart, kept me company. I only wish I could have shared it with Old Biddy to make her feel better.

In the days that followed the phone call, we both went through the motions and did our usual stuff together, but things were never really the same again. Not under the surface anyhow.

Old Biddy spent more time on the phone than she ever had before. We even had some visitors. Some of them smelled a bit like the nurses at the vet's, so I reckon they were from the doctor's surgery. This time it was Old Biddy's turn to be prodded and poked, but she took it in her stride. Didn't really change the smell, but for a while we all pretended nothing was wrong.

Then, one evening, after Old Biddy had spoken to someone again at length on the phone in the kitchen, she came over to me, and I could tell from the look on her face that we would talk at last. Well, Old Biddy would, and I would listen.

She sat me down on the sofa, took my face into her hands, so she could properly look me in the eyes, and said 'Oh, darlin', I *wish* things were different.

But they're not. Y' see, I'm quite sick, my darlin', and no two ways about it. And I'm getting sicker by the minute, so they tell me. Now, I've been trying to get my things in order, and that's all well and good. But y' see, there is one thing I still want to do before my time is up. I want to see the old country again. Y' know, the place where I grew up. I want to feel the mist and the rain again on my face before I have to go.'

And then she paused and added,' But don't y' fret, you're coming with me, darlin.'

I can't tell you how relieved I was when I heard her say that last bit. All the stuff she said before had had me mightily worried. I half expected her to tell me she was going to leave me with some strangers, or worse still, take me back to the horrible shelter. And I really don't think I could have coped with that.

I was so relieved she wasn't going to leave me behind, I didn't even mind when she took me to the vet's to get ready for the trip. Well, not much anyway. But she explained to me it was necessary, otherwise they wouldn't let me travel with her, so I didn't object too much.

The next few weeks flew by in a flurry of

'things to do before we leave'. I was well informed about what was going on because, in between bouts of terrible coughing, Old Biddy told me why she was doing what, and where. At length. I didn't do much. Just watched her get ready, and licked her hands and face a lot when she ran out of breath or coughed.

And in between worrying about Old Biddy and wondering what would happen next, I thought a lot about my parents. And missed them more than ever.

Then, one day, all suitcases were finally packed, the house was cleaned, and Old Biddy presented me with a brand new doggie travel crate. I can't say that I was massively excited about it – didn't really see the point of having it.

Old Biddy must have noticed the look on my face because she immediately apologised profusely. And then she explained that I *had* to use it because the people at the airline wouldn't let me travel in the airplane with her. Instead, I would have to travel inside the travel crate by myself in a different part of the plane.

I was even less excited about that, and only relented when she mentioned that this was the only way I could come with her.

However, what she didn't mention, was that it also involved ANOTHER trip to the vet's. Oh yes!!!

As soon as we arrived there, the vet just could not help himself and did his usual needle-sticking thing. I tried to think of other things, but the memory of my first trip on a plane with The Girlfriend popped into my head. That immediately got me worried again. I worried an awful lot until the vet was finished with me. Mainly about airports, and people stealing defenceless, woozy, little dogs inside silly bags.

This time, however, I needn't have worried. For starters I didn't get woozy or sleepy after the last injection. Mind you, when we finally got to the airport and I was manhandled away from Old Biddy and into the airplane via a cart that kept moving too fast, I almost wished I *had* been woozy. It really was frightening.

The only thing that kept me from trying to bust out of my crate were Old Biddy's last words before they took me away from her. As I told you, she always made sure to explain everything to me, and didn't treat me like I wouldn't understand – just because I am a dog and not a human.

This time was no different. Old Biddy explained to me – in detail – what would happen during the trip. And then she promised me 'hand on heart' to pick me up as soon as the airplane had landed.

A lot of the things were exactly how she'd explained them to me. Others not so much. For starters, she forgot to mention first how hot, and then how cold it would get where I was staying in the bowels of the airplane. And she also didn't mention how scary it all would be. And how loud! There was a lot of bumping and screeching and other majorly unpleasant sounds. They really made me want to pee quite badly. But no way was I going to disgrace myself and spend another trip sitting in my own pee. So I held it all in and waited anxiously for the time when I could finally get the hell out of my crate again.

Unfortunately it didn't happen for ages. The journey was positively endless.

Luckily the noises had more or less settled down to a constant droning after a while. And the movement settled down to a shudder, interrupted by the occasional drop that made my stomach almost pop out of my mouth.

Nope, I can't say that it was a great experience. Not by a long shot. Truth be told, I hated every single second of it and couldn't wait for it to be over already.

At some stage I must have drifted off unintentionally though despite my valiant effort to stay alert at all costs.

I was rudely awakened by a rumbling sound, followed by a loud screech and then an almighty bump that shook me all up, followed by more whooshing and screeching and shaking, until I thought the whole airplane was breaking apart.

I *nearly* peed myself right then after all, but just as I was getting dangerously close to losing control, we finally came to a shuddering halt. Then silence. And I could hear myself think again at last.

The ordeal wasn't quite over yet though, because the first person I saw after they opened the doors to wherever I was, wasn't Old Biddy at all. It was a man with a beard, who seemed pleasant enough, judging by the way he smelled and talked to me. But all I wanted was to see Old Biddy again.

When the man with the beard didn't open my crate, but put me in a car and drove me somewhere else, away from the airport, I *really* panicked. Surely this couldn't be happening to me again!!

Luckily it wasn't what I feared. But it wasn't great news either. I ended up at the vet's again – didn't I?!!!

I breathed a sigh of relief when all the vet did was check me all over and then call someone on the phone to tell them me and my paperwork were okay. Didn't know I had any paperwork, but there you go. I should have known by now that humans do a lot of weird stuff for no apparent reason.

And then, just as I was going into worry-overdrive once more, somehow miraculously, Old Biddy was finally by my side again. Clutching me to her closely. And apologising at length.

I decided to forgive her because nobody had stolen me this time. Nor, it turns out, had they stolen any of her suitcases and bags either. I spotted them piled high on a trolley before the vet put me on top of them, inside my crate once more. Because apparently dogs aren't allowed to walk inside a terminal by themselves. Yep, makes *noooooo* sense whatsoever!

I can't tell you how glad I was when we finally left the building and I was allowed to walk on my own four feet again!

I looked around, and then I sniffed the air to get my bearings… and almost did a double take.

Because to my utter surprise, there was *something* about the smell in the air… something that reminded me of *Home*. It wasn't exactly the same smell I remembered so well, but close, oh-so close. I got all excited. And then I started to shiver. Not from the excitement, but because it was bloody freezing. And that also reminded me of *Home*.

Old Biddy and I just stood there for a moment, in total silence, and took it all in.

It was cold, wet and miserable.

But we just couldn't stop smiling.

Chapter 9

HALF A WORLD AWAY

We stood side by side on the pavement outside the airport for quite a while, just taking it in, breathing deeply. Well, not for too long. Because by now I DESPERATELY needed to pee. Which I eventually did, at length, right next to where we were standing. Didn't even bother to find a tree – not that there were any in sight. Just let it go, I was that desperate. But Old Biddy didn't mind. She kept on smiling and patting my head, saying, 'There y' go, darlin'. You're such a good boy, my lovely.' Bit distracting when you are trying to pee, but I guess she meant well.

143

A little while later a car turned up and stopped right in front of us. The driver got out and greeted Old Biddy. He even said hello to me. From a distance.

I noticed the way he spoke sounded just like Old Biddy and not at all like the people back in Miami. But also not quite like most of the people who lived around my parents either. Similar though.

As I was pondering all this, the man grabbed all our suitcases and bags and put them into the boot of his car. And then, just as I was beginning to wonder if he was going to steal all our luggage after all, he stepped aside and opened the back door for us to get in. Old Biddy seemed okay with the arrangement, so I jumped in after her and sat down right beside her.

And off we went to wherever.

Not sure how long we drove, or in what direction. Why? Because I slept through the entire journey. I was so exhausted from the whole airplane trip from hell, I couldn't keep my eyes open any longer. Didn't even feel hungry, I was that tired. Also, being re-united with Old Biddy at last, I finally felt safe again. And so I made myself comfortable right next to her and fell asleep as soon as my head hit her lap.

And then I slept and dreamt until we got to where she wanted to go.

I must have been out for quite some time because, when the car stopped and I woke up, the sun – or whatever was visible of it amidst the mist and drizzle – was much lower in the sky.

I thought at first we had arrived where Old Biddy wanted to go to, but as she didn't make any move to leave the car, I could tell that wasn't the case. 'Hello, sleepyhead', she said, 'are y' feeling better now?' I licked her hand in response. But my stomach had begun to growl in earnest. I hadn't eaten a thing in a long while and my stomach knew it. Old Biddy laughed out loud when she heard it. And then she coughed, which really startled me and immediately made me very sad. Because, you see, I had been hoping with all my heart that coming over here meant Old Biddy's illness would just go away and leave us in peace. But of course I should have known better. It's just that Old Biddy was so happy now we were finally here, that the happy smell had been blocking the bad smell. But as soon as she coughed I could smell it again.

While all of this was racing through my head, I

almost missed that the driver had stepped out of the car. Not sure where he went, but when he came back, he handed Old Biddy a steaming paper cup with tea in it, and a bag full of food that smelled awfully nice.

She looked at me meaningfully and said, 'See, my darlin', I hadn't forgotten that y' must be famished by now.' And when she added 'Come on then!', I didn't need to be asked twice. I practically flew out of the car in my haste to get at the food she put into one of the bowls she had brought along.

I wasn't sure at first why we had to eat by the roadside – me on the pavement, and Old Biddy sitting sideways in the back seat of the car with her legs dangling down to the ground – but then she explained to me that dogs weren't allowed inside the pubs and restaurants along the way. I didn't really mind, as long as the food was good and there was lots of it. Luckily it was! And fortunately for us the rain had stopped so we didn't get soaking wet as we ate.

146

We didn't stay long after we had eaten, only for as long as it took Old Biddy to take me for a short walk across the car park so I could do my business. I didn't bother marking anything along the way because I got the impression we weren't going to hang around for much longer.

Afterwards, Old Biddy asked the driver to hold my lead for her because she needed to go find the bathroom for herself. I understood this. And that's the only reason why I stayed with driver. Didn't completely trust him, even though he hadn't done anything to give me reason not to. Figured, 'better safe than sorry', so I watched him all the time like a hawk, whilst we both waited for Old Biddy to return.

Fortunately she didn't take long. And then it was off to the car, and on with our journey. My tummy was happy at last, so I slept some more. And then I dreamt...

... the wind is blowing mightily and there is an unmistakable smell of salt and fish in the air, a smell so familiar I would recognise it anywhere in the world... seagulls are soaring and swooping and screeching up a storm above the angry sea... the waves fling mountains of white foam onto the pebbles and the wind rushes them further along...

... And that's when I suddenly spot them in the distance... my mum and my dad... and I know they are waiting for me, right there on the beach... I can see them

so clearly… my mum, smiling so much her face must ache, arms open wide, calling out to me… my dad laughing and picking up a pebble just for me… just the right size, too… and then I am running and running and running, and almost tripping over my own paws in my haste to get to them…

I woke up with a start because my nose was telling me that the smells from my dream were real. My heart began to gallop like mad and I almost fell off the seat in my haste to get to the window to see if it was right.

And yes, oh yes, there it was, the sea – just as my nose had been telling me. And the seagulls, exactly like in my dream!

And for one tiny, deliriously happy moment I believed that we had arrived back *Home*, and that Old Biddy's home and mine had miraculously turned out to be one and the same.

Only… we hadn't. And it wasn't.

Because when I looked closer, nose pressed tightly against the window, all I could see was a harbour with boats and ships of all shapes and sizes. And there was nothing about them that looked even vaguely familiar. Even the sea and the seagulls circling endlessly above, upon second glance, looked very different to the ones back *Home*.

I heard Old Biddy shout excitedly 'Look darlin', that's *Ros a Mhíl*! And there's the ferry that'll take us right back home to *Inis Meáin*. Y' know, the place

148

where I was born. The place where I first met Bertie!'

I was happy for her – I really was. But at the same time my heart ached somewhat fiercely because I realised I wasn't going *Home* after all.

And my next thought was, 'Oh no! Not a boat!' As if the airplane trip hadn't been bad enough.

But a boat it was. Well, a ferry, according to Old Biddy. Same thing really. Only bigger. And yes, no sooner had we set foot on it, than it started to heave. Just like my stomach.

The journey was as miserable as I'd imagined it would be. We sat on our seats, me halfway across Old Biddy's lap, wrapped up in some woollen blankets, a kind, burly man on the ferry had given to Old Biddy, seeing that we were both not used to the colder climate anymore.

Also, by now it was getting dark really fast. And that didn't exactly make things any better, because it meant that I couldn't see much and therefore couldn't distract myself from the constant rise and fall of the waves – *and* my poor stomach.

Fortunately, the ferry didn't take that long to get to the island Old Biddy was taking us to. Still, when we finally arrived, thoroughly frozen through by the sea breeze, we were both decidedly wobbly on our feet. Didn't stop Old Biddy from smiling though, and from touching the ground and whispering 'Home at last!' under her breath. And then her voice was getting really wobbly, too.

A little further away from the ferry we were met by a stranger in a car who seemed to have been waiting for us. As soon as he saw us he got out of his car and greeted Old Biddy. Can't tell you what was said and what was arranged, because Old Biddy had started to talk to him in a language I didn't understand a single word of. But the stranger must have understood because, at the end of their conversation, he picked up all our luggage and bundled it into his car. We got in the car right behind him, and then he took us to a tiny cottage, just over the hill. Not that we saw much of where we were going because by now it was almost completely dark outside.

Luckily it turned out to be only a very short journey. The shortest we had made so far. I was mightily relieved, I can tell you, because I REALLY wanted the whole trip to be over already.

The cottage was small and white, with dried grass on the roof. Not exactly sure why. Maybe they kept cows or goats up there.

As soon as we had arrived there, the driver got out of the car and picked up the keys to the cottage from under a flower pot. He also opened the front door for us, switched on the light and let us in. And then he carried all our luggage inside whilst we explored the living room and the tiny kitchen behind it.

I think Old Biddy offered to make him a cup of tea, because she was pointing at the cups in the kitchen as she was talking to him. But I can't be sure. Maybe she was just really wanting one for herself after all the travelling we had done.

Anyway, the driver left soon after that, and Old Biddy told me that this was the place we were going to stay at. It wasn't her old home – because that apparently had been sold a long, long time ago – but a place she had rented for us for the length of our stay. Luckily she remembered to switch languages again as she was explaining all this to me, otherwise I wouldn't have understood a word she said.

When she was done chatting to me, Old Biddy walked across the kitchen and opened a small door at the back of it. I followed her and we both stepped out into what turned out to be the back garden. Me to pee and poo and mark my territory, and her to take it all in, and breathe, *BREATHE* deeply. Without coughing once.

'Look at the stars, my darlin', will y' just look at the stars! I had all but forgotten how beautiful they are', she kept whispering as I was thoroughly marking the boundary walls of the garden.

We stayed outside a while longer, but finally turned in. When Old Biddy opened the fridge I noticed that there was a lot of yummy food in it – someone must have known we were coming.

We didn't eat much though. Well, Old Biddy didn't. And after our meal we took ourselves upstairs to the tiny bedroom and slept side by side in the bed with the huge flowery duvet.

Without waking up once during the night.

The next morning we had a *looooooong* cuddle in bed before we got up. Then we went downstairs and stepped out into the back garden once more. And, would you believe it, as soon as we did the sun came out. Just for Old Biddy. To welcome her home.

At least that's what she told me.

After breakfast, Old Biddy put on her walking shoes and off we went to explore the island. We didn't have far to go because it turned out to be very small, as I soon found out. I could have easily walked once around the whole island, and it still wouldn't have been as long a walk as the ones I had undertaken with my parents in my other life.

But the first thing we did that day was to walk down the road to a shop. I had to wait outside for Old Biddy, but that was okay because I could hear her talking excitedly inside the shop to someone. When she came out again, she was positively beaming. 'Oh, darlin', you would never believe it', she told me, 'my friend Mary still lives here. After all this time! And now we're going to visit her, if y' don't mind.'

To be honest, I don't really think it would have made much of a difference if I *had* minded, because there was nothing in this world that could have stopped Old Biddy from seeing her old friend again. But as it was, I was curious myself and didn't mind at all. Also, I figured, maybe there would be a treat in it somehow for me. Turns out there was. Mary gave it to me as soon as she and Old Biddy had stopped all the crying and the hugging that had started up as soon as we'd arrived at Mary's cottage.

Also turns out that Mary wasn't the only person left who knew Old Biddy from way back when. Over tea, they all turned up at Mary's cottage, in ones and twos, and there was a lot more crying and hugging, and holding hands, and shaking heads, and wringing caps – in the case of the only two men who came over.

I took all the stroking I received from everyone who arrived in my stride without flinching once. Because they were all very old and meant well. And because that way there were loads more treats to be had.

We stayed for hours. I finally fell asleep sometime between biscuits, lunch and afternoon tea.

I had never seen Old Biddy so happy before. Even though she kept crying on and off, during the telling of some story or other.

When they all stopped talking at last, we went back home, ate our dinner, and Old Biddy brought me up to speed with what had been said. She didn't talk as much to me as she normally did, because I think she was all talked out from chatting to her old friends, but I gleaned that we were going to meet them again over the next few days and weeks.

And that's exactly what happened.

We had a lovely time on the island of Old Biddy's youth. We went for walks every single day and visited 'all the old places' Old Biddy remembered so well. We walked past rows and rows of stone walls and old, abandoned cottages. And I marked them all, just to make sure we didn't get lost.

We also visited a strange ancient monument Old Biddy called *Dún Fearbhaí* a few times, where the stone walls were high and went around and around in a huge, endless loop. Took me ages to mark! Not exactly sure what it was, but Old Biddy had apparently met Bertie there in secret, back in the old days when they were courting. I think that's why Old Biddy kept stroking the walls. And once or twice, when she thought no one was looking, she kissed the stones.

We also visited the beaches on the island, one after the other. We had sandwiches on one beach in the sunshine, and got very wet from the rain and the wind on another. I got quite a bit of sand all over my fur and up my bottom that particular day. Tried shaking it off and, when that didn't work, tried licking it off. But that only made my tongue really gritty and got the sand stuck firmly between my teeth.

Old Biddy tried to help me by brushing it off, but that only helped to spread the sand all over the floor in the cottage. We even found sand in the bed the next morning!

The other thing we did a lot of was to meet up with Old Biddy's friends. And sometimes we shared our food with them. We even went to church on Sundays, and Old Biddy chatted away merrily with the old folks. I still didn't understand a word they said, but that was okay.

They had TONS of tea together, and biscuits, and cakes. And so did I. Well, apart from the tea. Never liked it much. But Old Biddy couldn't get enough of it. That was another thing she had in common with my mum.

Whilst all of this was going on, I was mostly left to rest and snooze under some table or other. I spent my time thinking a lot about my mum and dad while Old Biddy was busy catching up with her old friends and her memories. And I realised that, although I must be so much closer to my parents now, judging by the people and the smell of the land, this island was nowhere near where I had lived. And I couldn't tell Old Biddy, which meant that there was simply no way for me to find my *Home* again.

'So near and yet so far', my mum would have said. And she would have been right.

Still, despite all this, I had a right good old time on the island. And Old Biddy felt so much better for being back. She walked more, she coughed much less, and most of all she was happy. All the time. Even though the both of us weren't used to it being cold, wet and windy almost all the time any longer. Because when it was wet and windy back in Miami, it was still warm. And even though Old Biddy and I remembered the weather in this part of the world so well, our bones just didn't want to know.

Luckily, back at our cottage we had a fireplace

Old Biddy would light every morning and evening. And lots of thick, woollen blankets to wrap ourselves up in.

Old Biddy had taken to knitting in the evenings, and she even knitted a jumper just for me whilst we sat in front of the fireplace, huddled together, and watched the flames dance.

Unfortunately, as I once told you, all good things must come to an end. Bad things too, of course, but those you don't mind ending.

And so, one morning, I noticed that Old Biddy was smelling less happy than before and had taken to staring wistfully into the distance once more. And that's when I knew, even before she told me so, that our time on the island was coming to an end.

That day she took me to the beach one last time – the beach where she and Bertie had sat 'so many years ago' and had made a plan to leave all this behind. And to go on an adventure and start a whole new life for themselves, half a world away.

It wasn't raining that day, and the wind had calmed right down as we sat side by side on a grassy patch and watched the waves do their thing. And as Old Biddy stroked and kissed my head, she whispered in my ear, 'Almost time to go back now, darlin'. I just *wish* I had more time, but there y' go…' And then she asked me, 'One last dip?', and we walked right up to the water's edge and dipped our feet in the water. Even though it was icy cold.

And we both remembered.

We left the very next morning. And all the old folks came over one last time to say goodbye to us. Oh, and to give us all sorts of presents and trinkets. We sure left with a lot more luggage than we had arrived with! Then they all accompanied us down to the harbour where the ferry was already waiting for us. And every single one of them had tears in their eyes. Old Biddy did too. Because, you see, they all knew they would never see each other again.

When all the hugging and kissing goodbye was finally done, the old folks all watched us board the ferry.

And then they stood patiently on the quay below the ferry and waved, and wouldn't stop waving, as the ferry slowly left the harbour. They waved and waved, and Old Biddy waved back. Until they were tiny spots in the distance and she couldn't really see them clearly any longer.

Then she sat down. And I jumped up to sit on her lap to make her feel better.

My mum always used to say that one of the worst things in life is that, most of the time, you simply don't know when it's the last time you do something. Or see someone. You only know afterwards. When you can't go back and say goodbye properly. Which hurts a lot.

But this time the old folks and Old Biddy all knew that it was the last time. And it still hurt them a lot.

Old Biddy was crying silently as she watched her island vanish from sight. She didn't talk, but then no words were needed. I knew *exactly* how she felt.

I gave her lots of *mimos* and licked her face and hands an awful lot. So that she would feel better. So that she knew I would be there now to take care of her. Always. And I think she understood.

After a while I closed my eyes and let all the smells in the air drift over me. The sea that day was calm, and the sun had come out just for us, to wish us a happy journey – according to Old Biddy.

My stomach was deeply grateful as it didn't have to compete with the heaving of the ferry.

And then I only concentrated on Old Biddy's hands, stroking my head and back, never seeming to get tired with it. And in that moment I was happy.

I only opened my eyes when the ferry shuddered to a halt at last. We were still sitting down, but a long line of people had formed right in front of us, as keen to get off the boat as I was. And as I was staring at all the people, willing them to hurry up already, I suddenly saw a couple, right at the front of the queue. And they seemed awfully familiar…

At first I thought I was only imagining things, but then I looked again and my heart did this funny, painful little flip and then it almost stopped. Because the woman and the man laughed out loud and I would have recognised my mum and dad's laugh anywhere in the world.

I couldn't believe what my eyes and ears were telling me. But there they were, and now the breeze was wafting their hauntingly familiar smells over to me.

How could this be? After all this time and against all the odds, in a different country from our own, I had finally found my parents again. My wish had finally come true.

But you see, the funny thing with wishes is that they can twist away from you, and even when they do come true they often turn out differently from how you imagined them to be. My mum knows this, which is why she tells people to always makes sure to add 'only if it makes me happy' at the end of each wish they make.

I was so happy it completely froze me to the spot. And when I could move again, my parents were already walking away from me.

I barked, 'I am right here, Mummy!' and 'Wait for me, Papá!' And for a moment, they both stopped in their tracks and looked around searchingly.

But for some reason they didn't spot me.

I saw them look at each other wistfully and then slowly turn to walk away once more. It really made me frantic, and I was about to jump down from the Old Biddy's lap and run over to them at the speed of lightning, when it suddenly dawned on me that running over to my mum and dad would mean that I would have to leave Old Biddy behind forever and that I would never see her again.

And just like that I didn't know what to do.

I couldn't decide, nor could I move, and in the distance I saw my parents walking further and further away from me. My heart was aching so much it made me sick. And it would have been oh-so-easy to slip Old Biddy's frail old hands and make a run for it.

I saw the ramp of the ferry being lowered. The line of people kept moving and I watched my parents walk towards it hand in hand. I wanted to run over to them so badly, and at one point I actually turned around to Old Biddy to say goodbye.

But then she looked at me, and I think somehow she knew, because she said 'It's okay my lovely' and 'I love y' very, very much, my darlin'!'

And I simply couldn't do it.

Because, you see, I loved her too. And it was precisely at that moment I realised that she needed me so much more than my parents. And that even though they missed me like crazy, my mum and dad still had each other. But Old Biddy had no one in the world but me. And I simply couldn't bring myself to leave her, even though my heart was breaking in two.

And that's when I finally understood what they had told me over on the Other Side – you know, about life being all about learning and growing and doing something completely new. But even though I understood at last, it really hurt me, too. An awful, awful lot.

But then I remembered the song my mum had been listening to, over and over and over, right after I died, the one that goes '… it's not goodbye, it's just letting go for a little while…'

And so I let them go.

It was the hardest thing I ever did. I watched the people I loved most in the whole wide world walk out of sight and out of my life.

Because it was the right thing to do.

Because deep down I know this much is true, that somehow, somewhere, sometime we will meet again.

When the time is right.

Chapter 10

LAST MEMORY

What can I tell you about our journey back? Well, it turned out to be every bit as horrible as the last one. Only now it was even colder and more miserable for both of us because of all the goodbyes. Old Biddy was trying hard not to cry, and I was pining for my parents, knowing full well that every awful step of the journey back would take me further and further away from them.

We arrived back in what Old Biddy called 'the New World' in autumn. Well, it had been autumn in

Ireland. Cold, misty, and drizzly right up to the very end of our journey. Back in Miami it was hot and humid, and you couldn't even tell summer had left. I didn't mind though because my heart was still aching so very much over my parents, I didn't need aching bones on top of it.

And even though I could tell that a big part of Old Biddy's heart had stayed behind in the country of her birth, she also seemed to be relieved to be back in the warmth once more.

We were both numb for a while, but then we slid right back into our daily routine. Both lost in our thoughts a lot, but happy to be in each other's company. And for the longest time we just ignored what was coming and pretended that all was well again.

We had two more lovely summers and winters together. Easy years. Just comfortable, without any ups and – most importantly – without any downs.

But even so, almost imperceptibly, our walks were getting shorter again, and our pace just that little bit slower. And this time it wasn't me who was slowing us down. Well, not at first. But then, all of a sudden, my legs started to give out again. Only from time to time, but enough to tell me that it wasn't just Old Biddy's time that was coming to an end.

Old Biddy didn't notice at first because she was too busy trying to hide her nasty coughs from me. But when she did notice at last – around the time I got the horrible pain in my back again that made me whimper out loud – she looked at me, and I could tell from her look that she finally understood.

And I bet, she could tell the same from mine.

After that we didn't hide stuff from each other any longer. After all, what's the point?! We just shared a lot of *mimos* and did every little thing we could together.

No more trips to the doctor for her, no more trips to the vet for me.

167

I stayed with Old Biddy right until the end. Well, *almost* right until the very end.

Because she had the kindness to let me go first.

So I wouldn't have to end my days old and sick in a shelter and die among strangers after she had gone. So I wouldn't have to spend the time I had left in misery without her.

The vet came over, but I wasn't scared. I understood. I just kept looking at Old Biddy, and she kept stroking me and telling me she loved me, right there by her side, in her bed, until it was all over.

And I repaid her kindness by waiting for her over on the Other Side.

Picked her right up, when her time on earth finally came to an end, too.

She didn't take long to arrive either – although it's hard to say exactly how much time had passed, because of that weird time-stretching thing between the Other Side and the world of the living I once told you about.

But it can't have been more than a day or so.

And I met Bertie, too, whilst I was waiting for her. He was as nice as she had told me he was. And he was mightily impatient for Old Biddy to come over at last. So they could be back together again.

I did a proper little happy dance when Old Biddy finally came over to the Other Side. And so did she.

And then we got to say goodbye again. Because the link to my parents had already begun to pull me right back home once more.

But this time it wasn't sad to say goodbye, and Old Biddy didn't mind. She was happy now she had her beloved Bertie back and would never be lonely again.

The last thing I remember is her telling me that she was so very glad she had met me. I felt the same, but before I could tell her so, there was an almighty wrench…

And I was back.

Chapter 11

HOME

It was a beautiful day and the little puppy sniffed the crisp spring air.

It knew exactly what it wanted. It always had.

Only this time I remembered.

Everything.

Right from the start.

There was a distinct, almost human smile on its roguish little face as it was staring at the door. Everything was going to be alright at last.

Because I just *knew* that today was the day when I would finally be with my mum and dad again.

No doubt at all.

None.

Whatsoever.

But I better run now.

Things to do, places to see, trees to mark, a whole new life to live, and tons and TONS of *mimos* to be had.

THE END

ALSO BY MARTINA MARS

If you haven't read the first two books in the series yet, you can catch up with what went on before in the life (and death) of Nelson and his family in:

I AM NELSON
The story of a little dog who is larger than life. Even when he's dead.

and

I AM NELSON - What Happened Next
The story of the little dog continues. Still dead. Still as alive as ever.

www.martinamars.com

****

If you would like to stay in touch and find out first about any offers and future book releases, please join my readers' list and get your own **FREE** copy of

My Brother Alfred
A little Scottie dog finds his forever home. A short story

here:

www.martinamars.com/free-ebook

AUTHOR'S NOTE

This book could be easily summed up like this: I couldn't wait any longer for Nelson to return, so I wrote him back.

And yes, that makes this book a work of fiction. All the locations exist, but my book is only loosely based on them. I have used the R. Hardy Matheson Preserve in Miami, Florida as inspiration for the park Nelson ends up in after he escapes the shelter, but it doesn't resemble it completely.

I am aware that there are quite a few animal shelters near that park, but the one I am describing in this book exists only in my imagination. As do all the characters and events in the story, with the exception of Nelson's family and friends and everyone else who has been mentioned in the memoirs *I AM NELSON* and *I AM NELSON - What Happened Next*.

The only event that really took place is the one involving Nelson's Auntie Pachy in Chapter 1.

Right after Nelson's first book *I AM NELSON* came out, the idea for a possible trilogy briefly crossed my mind.

I dismissed it pretty much immediately because, in all honesty, I never really intended to write a second book. Never mind a third.

But then… I did.

Nelson kept nudging me and I just couldn't help myself.

I AM NELSON - What Happened Next was released in September 2022, and once again, I didn't really intend to write another book because I very much felt that, short of Nelson being born again and miraculously finding his way back home to us, this would be the end of my writing about/for him. I even put words to that effect into my notes at the back of the book.

Only then, one day, the first sentence for a potential third book suddenly popped into my head and simply refused to go away again. It happened right in the middle of my dabbling with writing something in a completely different genre, and completely stopped me in my tracks. Because that's exactly what had happened with Nelson's first two books. In both cases, the first sentence appeared in my head and then persuaded me to start writing them in the first place.

However, this time around I didn't want to give in and write the book because Nelson had not come back and I really didn't want to write something that wasn't true.

But then something peculiar happened. My sister-in-law called me one day from Buenos Aires in Argentina and told me she thought she had seen Nelson. She was so sure it was him in another dog's body, she even sent me a picture of the little dog in question. Unfortunately she then immediately lost track of him and never saw the little dog again after that, so we will never know if it was Nelson or not.

But it left me wondering: *what if* she was right and Nelson *had* been reborn, not close to his old home, but somewhere far away, and couldn't find his way back home. And out of this '*what if*' the idea for a third book was born. I still didn't want to write it because I felt I'd rather wait and see if Nelson would come back for real, and also because I felt crossing from memoir into fiction wasn't such a great idea. But the more I mulled things over, the greater my urge to write it anyway became. I then spent quite some time telling myself – and all my friends and family – that I was only writing this as an exercise for myself, to see if I could write fiction.

Much of the book strangely wrote itself – I can't describe it any better way. Whenever I planned for the story to go in a certain direction, or for Nelson to travel to a particular country, something always stopped me writing it. And I was as surprised at the twists and turns in the book as everyone else. Right down to many of the locations that to my utter surprise turned out to look exactly how I had described them, when I researched them *afterwards*.

I also remember one incident in particular, when I was writing about Nelson's time with Old Biddy. In my head I suddenly heard her say something in

Irish to him. Now, I don't speak any Irish, so I had to look it up, and I was stunned to find that not only was it pronounced exactly the way I had heard it in my head, but that the translation of it meant what I had thought it would.

Of course, Nelson would now say, 'You really should know by now that my mum is weird'. And I guess, you could say that he is right…

To cut a long story short, I kept on writing until I finally finished Nelson's unexpected 'what-could-have-been' story in spring of this year. And when I read and re-read it, I decided that it would make a fitting end to Nelson's story after all, never mind that it's fiction.

Want to know something else that is strange?

Whenever I write, I keep snippets of ideas in a notebook for future reference. And just now, as I was looking for a fitting end to this note, I came across something I had written on Nelson's behalf just before I embarked on writing this book. It goes like this:

'My mum will never be completely sure if any of this really happened – but then you can never be 100 percent sure of anything, this side of things. But deep down she knows…'

Hastings, 25th July 2023 – which of course would have been Nelson's birthday

ACKNOWLEDGMENTS

I would like to thank all my friends and family for bearing with me when I talked for hours on end about writing *yet another* dog book. Thanks for not being bored stiff with it all – or at least doing a good enough acting job so I didn't notice – and for your unwavering interest that never ceases to amaze me!

Thanks also to everyone who read Nelson's books and wrote to me over the years – I was very touched by all your kind comments. Thank you for continuing to share Nelson's journey!

And *muchas, muchas gracias* to Auntie Pachy! For calling me that day and telling me you were sure you had seen Nelson. Without you I would have never written this book.

Another huge thank-you goes to my fabulous launch teams in the UK and the US, and to Uncle Richard and Auntie Dee, for your most helpful comments that really made a difference! And to Fiona Wilson, who most diligently spots and corrects any mistakes in my books, ditto! Any remaining errors are Nelson's or my own.

And lastly, I would like to thank my husband Polo Piatti for all the beautiful melodies that bring back memories of Nelson time and time again, and for waiting and hoping with me. You once told me to never give up, and I won't.

Bye-bye, Nellie! Until we meet again. Thanks for making me write your story. I hope you remember the music and it keeps you good company wherever you are...

ABOUT THE AUTHOR

Martina Mars is an actress and former dancer and as such has had all the usual – and unusual – daytime jobs in her time. She fully expected her first book also to be her last, but found out to her great surprise that writing is compulsive, and she hasn't stopped writing since. She lives with her husband in East Sussex in the UK.

www.martinamars.com/contact

Printed in Great Britain
by Amazon